Make 'Em Beg to Be Your Client!

The Nonfiction Authors'
Guide to Selling, Serving,
and Funding a Movement

DR. ANGELA E. LAURIA

DIFFERENCE
PRESS

Difference Press

McLean, Virginia, USA

Copyright © Angela Lauria, 2018

Difference Press is a trademark of Becoming Journey, LLC

Published 2018

ISBN: 978-1-68309-227-8

Cover Design: Michelle Grierson

Editor: Kate Makled

Author's photo courtesy of M. Douglas Silverstein

This one is for the members of The Order of the Quill.

Thank you for SEEING me.

Thank you for begging to be my clients.

Thank you for trusting me with your books.

Every day we work together you inspire me to step more fully into my own gifts, so I can be worthy of having clients as smart, heart-centered, magical, loving, and life-changing as each of you are.

TABLE OF
CONTENTS

INTRODUCTION

"P.S. I need space."

He broke up with me over email… in a P.S.

It was 1996 and I was 23 when it happened and I never thought I would get over it.

At the time, I was working for New York Times best-selling author, David Wise. Wise wrote about spies and hired me for 4 hours a day as a researcher and editor. I'd cry all the way from my apartment in Alexandria Virginia to his office in downtown DC and then, for 4 merciful hours, I'd be lost in the world of espionage.

My work was intense and high-stakes. My boss had no tolerance for drama or distraction. But then, at 2pm, when my work day was done, I'd be back in my teal 1994 Dodge Shadow crying again.

In the evenings, I was an Actor's Equity Stage Manager for professional theatre companies in DC. Usually there was a gap of about 5 hours between 2pm when my book job would end and 7pm when my theatre job would start. Rehearsal often went until midnight or beyond so by the time I got home, I would pass out from the long day, but the window from 2pm to 7pm was pure torture.

Most days I'd curl up in a ball and cry the whole time. But on good days, I'd make it to the floor of the self-help section of the Borders Book Store in Bailey's Crossroads, just a few minutes from my house. The store was closed down almost a decade ago now, but I'm still sure I could navigate my way to my well-worn spot on the ground blind folded.

Self-help books were my first, last, and only resort. I made $200 a week from my book job and about $235 a week from my theatre job. That was $1740 a month total and my rent alone was $860. I didn't have money for therapy, but somehow, I could swing books.
I read about 1 a day in that window of time. And there was something else I discovered at that book store – self-help tapes!

Marianne Williamson had a collection of tapes on relationships, money, happiness, you name it. I bought them all. And driving to work I would listen to them over and over. I still have most of those tapes memorized. I listened to them so many times, Marianne sort of became a part of me, like the wise older aunt I never had.

Her tape on relationships was the hardest for me to listen to because I had to imagine being with someone other than this Australian surfer dude who broke my heart. Marianne asked her listeners to make a list of all the attributes of the person you wanted to spend your life with. My attributes were really just a description of him, since all I wanted was to get him back.

Tall, long--hair, bare foot, nature-lover, Aussie accent, amazing kisser….

And then, just as the list would crystalize, Marianne asks:

"Now…" (dramatic pause) "Would he date you?"

#micdrop

Marianne is the queen of the mic drop and her point was well taken. The woman he wanted to be with was a barefoot, nature-loving, Aussie surfer; not a theatre girl in a big city located hours from a crappy beach, never-mind a beach with good surfing.

Marianne was right! I was NOT the person that guy would be with.

And so, I was left with a choice: Become someone else or become more of me.

It wasn't easy, but I chose me.

I loved DC and books and libraries and museums and theatres. I was a city girl. I WORE SHOES… like, all the time. I was not going to be happy in the bush in Western Australia. I SLOWLY began to see, I was not the right girl for the Australian guy. More than that, Marianne taught me that I needed to get clear on who I was to even know who the right guy for me might be. The process took another 7 years.

I share this story about my early dating life here, because it's the basis for this book. To get people to BEG to be your client, you have to first be the person they would be begging. As Marianne said on that tape "You have to become the person you want to attract."

And that is the message of this book at its heart. You can't expect your clients to beg you to help them until you become the person who is worthy of getting begged.

Here's a short quiz to give you a sense of how ready you are to be the person who regularly is begged by total strangers to take their money and help them solve a problem.

Make 'Em Beg to Be Your Client Quiz

T | F - I'm 100% sure what I am/or want to be "The Best in the World" at.

T | F - I'm 100% sure of the problem I solve for my clients (in their words not mine).

T | F - I'm 100% sure the result I get for my clients.

T | F - I'm 100% sure what I do works and works reliably for clients who follow my framework.

T | F - I have generated multiple tens of thousands of dollars in booked revenue.

T | F - I have lots of case study clients who came with the same problem and left with the same solution. (It's okay if they are anonymous but they have to be real clients you can call to mind).

Until you have a perfect score on that quiz, you will not have a steady flow of clients begging to work with you; but don't worry because in this book I am going to teach you how to get there as quickly as possible. Often it takes my clients just 90 days! And (spoiler alert) the answer is not to do more work, it's to do less!

It turns out the answer to getting clients begging to work with you is pretty similar to meeting the right guy.

Step 1: Know yourself

Step 2: Be yourself

Step 3: Open your heart & shine

Imagine there was some playbook to teach you how to manipulate someone into loving you. Would you want to win a partner that way? How long do you think that relationship would last?

Getting clients to beg to work with you isn't about manipulation or trickery. It's about knowing who you are, showing up fully, and being the person your prospects KNOW will be the answer to a prayer.

So, before we get started, take out a sheet of paper and make a list of your ideal client, the one you most want to help, to teach and to serve…. And then ask yourself:

Would she beg to work with you?

CHAPTER 1

Book to Booked

"Can I talk to you for a minute?" Myrna said
quietly.

I stepped away from my desk and walked with
her to a quiet corner on the ballroom level of
The Author Castle, away from the bustle of our
book launch event.

"I know I'm supposed to be happy today, with my
book launching, but something feels *off*. I love
starting projects, often complicated projects,
like quilts. I love learning new techniques and I
thrive on challenges. I think it's pretty fair to say
I haven't quite figured out the *finishing* part.

So, writing a book – and finishing it – has been *huge* for me. It was important to break the unfinishing cycle. I loved the process, the accountability, the peer pressure, and the expectation held that it would be finished – *on time*. But now, it feels like my kid left for college. It's a sudden release from the constraints and I'm distracted by the sudden reduced sense of pressure. It's disorienting, and I'm not sure what to do next."

Another "victim" of what I call Post-Book Depression.

Here's the pattern: Getting the book accepted is euphoric. Writing the book is hard but feels important – so our other priorities are put on hold. The editing is grueling and feels like it will never end. You have coached yourself through it all to get to this moment…and now that big day arrives. *You* are an *Author*. It feels good for about three seconds and then you start to have a total melt down.

What was I thinking?

Can I really handle this?

Do I have what it takes to be an author?

This is a lot of responsibility!

What do I do next?

Suddenly, the challenge of *writing* a book seems so much more fun and achievable than the challenge of *marketing it*. It's like taking your first baby home from the hospital and feeling as though you have to figure out everything about being a parent, overnight!

The Numbers Don't Add Up

I started The Author Incubator in February of 2013. By the time I opened the doors, I had 19 years of experience in the publishing industry behind me. But those 19 years were spent in the "old" publishing world. The world where publishers placed bets on authors and hoped their resulting books would sell. If they did, the author would get more offers, from the publisher, if not, the author would go back to hunting for another great idea and have to pitch it to publishers all over again.

It was the *idea* that would sell books or not, not the *author*. Oh sure, there were press releases and book signings that the author would create and hold, but that didn't really move the needle on sales, or author careers. In that world, books were judged as being "good" if they sold, and if they sold well, it was because of the underlying ideas behind them. In any case, for most of the authors I worked with in the 90s and 00s, the next step after publishing a book was writing the next one, and hoping and praying for strong sales, and that the publisher would foot the bill for the ideal store placements.

This approach worked for very few authors back then, and it works for a lot fewer now. These days, unless you are launching a political campaign or celebrity tell-all, books will sell because the *authors* sell them. There is no shortage of marketing advice for new nonfiction authors, but sadly, most of it is based on an old system and it doesn't work for most authors. Such bad advice falls into two primary categories:

1. Do more stuff
2. Sell more books

"Do more stuff" advice is all focused on tactics — encouraging the author to spend all their time hustling to be interviewed on podcasts, creating social media conversations, giving speeches, sending postcards, calling libraries, and building huge lists to get the word out about their book release. The problem with the "do more stuff" approach is most authors can't actually do those things well. There just isn't enough time or money, and they don't have the skills or relationships in publicity or communications, so what they do isn't terribly effective.

"Sell more books" advice goes back to the way traditional publishers make money. Generally, publishers take about 90% of the revenue from a book, so the way *they* make more of it is by focusing authors on efforts that result in selling books. Authors don't even get much of a discount when buying copies of their own books, because publishers make a big chunk of change from the author's purchase – after all, the authors are the most likely customers to buy it.

My advice is the direct opposite:
1. Do less stuff (and do it better)
2. Give away your books (and make money from clients)

Of course, most traditional publishers and traditional book marketers think I'm out of my mind, but the way I see it, there is no way to get the numbers to add up in their model. Authors make somewhere between $1 and $10 per book. There is still no way to sell enough books to really thrive as an author, let alone fund a movement. Unless you are a celebrity or a politician, there just aren't enough hours in the day to make "doing more stuff" or "selling more books" pay off.

Now, you can go and built a platform and get famous with or without your book, but that would also take a lot of time, money, and luck. So, sure, work on it, but there is a much easier way to make money from a book: Give it away and focus on selling your coaching or consulting services to readers.

This is a business model that works well – and consistently – and I'm going to teach you how in this book.

The average author makes less than $250 from their book, but *our* average author makes $60,000 from their book – AVERAGE! And we have many authors who make $60,000 (or more) a MONTH, every month, after their book is out. You can have that too, but you have to be open to a totally new model for converting a book to generate revenue.

I should say, there is nothing wrong with making $250 from your book. You don't *have* to use a book to build your business and fund your movement. A book can be a beautiful creation or catharsis experience that never goes beyond that, and that's also okay. But if you picked up this book, it's probably because you *want* to have a business where you help amazing people and businesses transform to the next level.

There are the steps you will need to take externally, and then there are the internal adjustments you will need to make, in order to become the person who has the outcome you want.

I checked in with Myrna a few weeks after her launch, and she said:

"I suspect you have known this all along. I have had an inner conflict going for some time, and this is the real reason I haven't signed a coaching client, the reason I have self-sabotaged in the past. I am fearful, which I believe is some scarcity mindset.

I have been dividing my energy, because I am too afraid to let go of the one business success that I have had after several failures.

It is so very clear to me now that all of my energy has to be focused in one direction. Now I have to figure out how to do that. How do I let go of the one success I have had? How do I trust that my coaching business will be a success? How do I stop what I am presently doing – which includes leading a team of people – in order to do what I am supposed to be doing? When I say 'supposed to be doing,' I mean the work I know is what God has told me to do, has called me to.

I am not so much of a woo woo person, but I do know about energy and vibration, the Bible, and even general logic – and they all agree that a house divided cannot stand!

I have been stepping back and observing what I am doing, and why I am not having success, and conclude this is the reason. Now I need help figuring out how to let go of the one and grab a hold of the other. How do I let go of the 'child' I know and love to nurture the 'child' I know is being created?"

If you are reading this, I bet parts of her story feel familiar for you. The risk of letting go of what you have today feels more tangible than experiencing the upside of what you want. And so, you stay stuck. The book itself can't unstick you, not my book nor your completed book. Only *you* can unstick you. The advice I can give you in doing so will include a combination of strategies, tactics, and tools for managing the drama.

You can also decide to be happy with what you have now. A book on a shelf is still a fantastic accomplishment. Or you can decide to take it all to the next level – to reach more people, to expand your platform, to become to most potent and impactful version of yourself.

Myrna asked: "How do I let go of one and grab for the other?" I wrote this book as my answer to her, and for all the other difference-making authors out there. People who wrote a book because they wanted to make a bigger difference, but they are afraid that somehow going for the next level means they will have to give up what they already have.

In this book, you will learn the exact steps and strategies to:

- Get your book into the hands of the right people, those who are most ready to put your ideas and strategies into action;

- Make more money (while helping people get amazing

   results) so that you can fund your dreams, and make the

   difference you were born to make;
- Stop spinning your wheels trying to figure out how to design a business you are proud of;
- Attract prospects who ask you if you will work with them, instead of the other way around; and
- Let go of the need to convince, prove, or show people that you are good at what you do.

If you already have a book, and it's not getting you clients like you hoped (or if you want to write a book that gets clients begging to work with you), this book is for you.

CHAPTER 2

Your Wee Portal

When I created The Author Incubator, I wanted to make it really easy for authors to work with me. I launched with three complementary programs to address all the needs and questions I commonly heard from first time authors. The first program was called Free Your Inner Author, and it was designed to help you write your book. The second was called Difference Press, and it was an editing and self-publishing service to help you get your book published on Amazon. The third was called Coaches' Book Circle, and it was for authors who wanted help promoting their books. That was it! *Write! Publish! Promote!*

And a program to guide you in each. Essentially, my first business was a way of helping first time or frustrated authors do all the things the old publishing model called for, using some new tools and my guidance.

I imagined people who didn't have a book yet would join Free Your Inner Author, and then ascend to Difference Press to publish it, and then elect to join the Coaches' Book Circle to build a business around the book. And if they *did* have a finished book already, they could join later along the ascension trail. I figured no one could be confused, right? I'd just ask where they were in the book process, and slot them into the right program for them.

I launched on February 7, 2013.

By the summer, I was interviewing for corporate jobs.

I had made a handful of sales, but it was feeling random. I'd close one here, close another there. Mostly, I was spending a lot of time talking to people on the phone who *said* they wanted to buy from me, but never seemed to *actually* buy. Very often, what they did buy from me would be a custom offering. So, I added one on one coaching sessions for $150 an hour to my site, and called that my fourth offering.

The problem, which I didn't realize at the time – and it turns out most coaches *never* realize – is that running a business with four separate offers is like running four separate businesses. The financials are different, the staffing is different, the procedures are different, the marketing process is different, the sales call is different. And what's worse, there was no clear indication for what I was the best in the world at, nor who my ideal client could be. Was I just great at everything book-related? I didn't have a clear way to decide who was a fit for my program, because I thought I wanted to work with everyone at every stage. I made it hard for my clients to tell if I was a good fit for them, because I was trying to keep too many options open. I remember, on so many phone calls, I would ask my client to tell me what they were looking for –

and then I would give them examples of how I'd done stuff like that before, and why I would be a good person for them to hire to do it. I think I thought every sales call was a job interview!

This all changed in August 2013. I had gone for an *actual* job interview at a major communications firm in the DC area. It was the dream job. It was close to my house, easy commute, gorgeous building, fat $250K a year salary. I'd been trying to get this particular head hunter to place me for an interview for a long time, and he wouldn't give me the time of day. Now, finally, he got me an interview – and it was a "perfect fit." The interview did go really well…

Except for my breathing problem.

Throughout the interview, it felt like an elephant was pausing briefly on my chest. I just couldn't take a full breath of air in. In spite of it, I still managed to sell the leaders on my many accomplishments and showcase how I would be an asset to the organization. The interview lasted four hours, and as I walked out of the building toward my car, I finally took that full breath. I was free! I couldn't wait to get back to my real life!

The phone rang before I even made it to my car, and it was the headhunter. I fumbled for my phone, and then found myself puking all over my hand.

"Maybe I'm getting sick," I thought, as I searched for wipes in the glove compartment.

But I knew I wasn't getting sick. The thought of leaving my dream business to take a corporate job had *made* me sick. And now, I was about to burn a bridge I'd been building for three years.

I sat in the parking lot and redialed the headhunter.

"Steve? Hey, it's Angela."

He asked how it went.

"Great interview," I said. "These guys are awesome. My sense is they will want to make an offer — and I should give you a heads up now, it's not a fit for me."

Steve was not happy. And I get it. He had vetted me, he sold me in to the client. I said I was interested, and now he has to go back to the client and try to sell someone new. I felt responsible for wasting all their time. He hung up politely and professionally, but I figured I'd just blown the last shot I had at getting back in to a corporate job.

I opened the car door and threw up one more time.

My credit cards were maxed, my cash flow was not flowing, and I just turned down a $250K a year job. I hit the wall.

Right there… in that wall… was the thing I'd been missing this whole time.

A wee portal.

A wee portal is a small, yet clearly defined, entry point for a prospect.

Until that day, I'd had sort of a business "jungle." When a prospect would get on a call with me, I'd tell them all about the jungle, and they would agree it sounded splendiferous! For sure, it was a place they would someday like to visit. But they were not sure how exactly to get there, or what exactly they would do when they got there, or, frankly, if it would be any good. It was too abstract and too unknown for them.

When I found my wee portal, my prospects could know the location and the mode to enter into my world. There was a doorbell they could ring, and when I flipped the latch, I could let them in, or not! I became the Queen of the Castle (long before I knew I'd end up living in a castle). When I *did* decide to open the door and invite them in, there was a pretty little mat and a coat rack where they could wipe their feet when they entered. Everything would make sense, and the experience would be familiar.

I discovered all of this quite by accident or more accurately, out of desperation. I could not afford my mortgage.

I'd never missed a mortgage payment before, and I didn't really want to find out what happens when you do. So on August 15th, just two weeks before my next mortgage payment was due (for which I did not expect to have the money), I wrote this email:

Hi Angela,

There's an exciting trend in publishing and I want to make sure you are in on it -- **Kindle Singles**. Have you been following this?

Kindle Singles have been out for a couple years as a format, but they seem to have hit the tipping point about two weeks ago when an interview with Barack Obama took the marketplace by storm. The President visited Amazon and, while there, was interviewed by the Kindle Singles editor, David Blum. **Singles have now sold over 6,000,000 copies and authors of Kindle Singles are making real money -- on average Kindle Singles authors make roughly $22,000, per book!**

And these books are short -- just 5,000 to 30,000 words (about 20-120 pages).

How cool would it be to make $22,000 for writing 20 or 30 pages?

But there's a catch. Kindle Singles is very selective about who they publish. They get about 1,000 submissions a month and only a few are selected for publication. So, these need to be very high-quality books. I've figured out some of the criteria they use to make their decision, but now I'm trying to figure out the exact formula for what gets selected and I really need your help.

I'm looking for 5 people who want to write a short book within the next 90 days.

I will help you write your book and I'll work with you to get it published -- ideally by Kindle Singles. As a publisher, I have a considerable number of resources and information about Kindle Singles which I'd like to leverage in this short window of time and see if I can crack the code so I can help more people write Kindle Singles. **If you are interested in getting a small book done and published this year,**

please reply with a description of your idea or an explanation of why you'd like to work with me. This is a very unique opportunity to get in on a new trend early, without having to do all the heavy lifting yourself -- and even if you don't get picked up by Kindle Singles, we will still publish your ebook on Kindle and iBooks, so you can sell your work and help people with your message.

I hope you are as excited about Kindle Singles as I am. We have reached the tipping point and there is a chance to make real money and a real impact with a very short book! I can't wait to work with you on yours!

Let's do this!!

Angela

Within an hour, 100 people had lined up behind my wee portal. I had not had 100 people express interest in anything I had done up to that point. I wrote back with more details and the cost, which would be $1,000, to be paid in full up front. I wanted to start this work with just five people, but ten clients actually made the payment within minutes of getting my reply. I didn't really think through the implications of including my PayPal link in the email.

I closed the latch, leaving a line outside, and cozied up with my first ten clients to create the program that has evolved to be The Author's Way. Sure enough, in 90 days, all ten books were published.

So, what was the wee portal?

It was a very clear and specific result, with a very clear and specific deadline, and with a very clear and specific leader (Notice, that leader was *me!* Not the client!)

People did want to come to the jungle, but until I sent that message, no one knew how to get in. It was like a beautiful private property that people admired from afar but had no road access.

Before you can have clients begging to work with you, you *have* to identify your wee portal. And, I know you are going to want to argue with me on this one, but if you try to have more than one wee portal you will make being successful so much harder – for all the reasons my four separate offers didn't work.

The great thing about your wee portal is that you don't have to spend a whole bunch of time and money at the outset building it, and you certainly don't have to have it all figured out before you sell it. You just need to write the marketing for it (for me, it was this one email you see above) and go find clients to fill it. The magic is to give yourself permission to *create* the program *with* your first clients. In exchange for being part of the development, they will get an incredible deal and a lot of your personal time and attention – so it's a win-win.

I got home from that job interview at 4pm on a Wednesday, and this program was created, the email was written and coded, and it was mailed out to my list at 2:44pm on Thursday. By Friday, I had $10,000 in my PayPal account. Do not make this more complicated than it is. Spending lots of time trying to get this stuff "right" actually makes it less right, as ironic as that is.

The wee portal is the specific result you can get with someone in the next 90 days. If you are having trouble identifying your wee portal, here's an exercise for you: Look at social media and magazines, or do some internet searches, and see if you can find examples of other people's wee portals in your space. Try to find 10 wee portals. I promise they are out there. Do a little analysis or inventory about what you like and don't like about the results they promise. Could you get that result for your clients? Have you gotten it for yourself?

When I created the offer you see here, I didn't entirely know *how* I was going to deliver the result. There was no workbook, no videos, no event, no canned tactics. My only plan was to use email and the phone. That's the way I had done everything at my job. When I had any project for work, I would simply email people or call them. I didn't have an outline or a plan, didn't know exactly what I'd do this week or next. I just knew I would work with my new clients, over the phone and email, to create and publish their books – and take a lot of notes about the things I did along the way that made their results easier to achieve.

You should not be filming anything or having anything designed. You don't need a program name. You don't need a logo. You need *a result*.

Everything you sell, or think about selling, outside of your wee portal will have a high hidden cost to it. That would be the massive opportunity cost inherent in your choice against developing that one product, that repeatable result, and building a tremendously sane and stable, cash-flowing business out of it. Every minute you spend away from your wee portal, you're distracted, and that means you are not learning the things you need to learn in order to "fail" in a meaningful way.

If you ever listen to a high performer like Richard Branson or Elon Musk speak, when they're talking about the notion that their biggest success came from failing, they don't mean "failing" as in trying to figure shit out, or failure to launch. What they mean is that they launched a rocket, and that rocket blew up, and somebody died. That's what *they* mean by failing. First they had to build an actual rocket. And in order to get *there* they had to hire people, design a rocket, secure loans to build the rocket, get permission for the rocket to go up in the air, and then the rocket had to explode – and someone had to die. That's what they mean by "failing."

They do not mean "sitting on the couch (or in a board meeting), trying to figure out how to launch a rocket." If you think you are qualifying for the "failing fast" awards while you spend all your time trying to figure it out, let me assure you, you are not. If you are my client, I would much rather have you fail at getting nine clients by the end of this quarter, because say we're going to do a sprint, these nine weeks of program are going to inform your sprint, and I would much rather see you "fail" in not getting to that goal of nine clients – after you've made 100 sales calls over the next 9 or 12 weeks – than "fail" by spinning your wheels trying to figure it out for 12 weeks. That's the difference between passive action and *massive action*.

Now here's the thing, having a wee portal doesn't feel as sexy as glitzy tactics or prestigious visibility — like being invited to speak at a conference, or something like that. What a lot of my eager clients often want to do, as it's expressed to me, sounds like *I want to do this fun stuff and so I'm going to do all this fun stuff and it's going to magically turn into clients* — and the truth is, it doesn't magically turn into clients at all.

It's so key to know that you have to *start with revenue*. When you start with revenue, everything else becomes much easier. Your goals don't have to be crazy, but you do have to achieve some consistent revenue to do anything you want to do (other than get a job instead of build your business), and to get to consistent revenue, you need to pick one wee portal and work it.

Seth Godin books are really good for inspiration. He talks a lot about "shipping." What he means by shipping is putting stuff out there – notice, he's not figuring it out but putting it out, actually taking massive action – and then making adjustments. One of the reasons you might not be selling your program today is doubt, for instance maybe you won't be able to sell it. That self-talk sounds like, "so let me just reject myself in advance and then I won't do pick the wee portal so that I won't find out that I can't sell it." Maybe you're afraid you're not going to do a good job, or your client is not going to get the results. You're thinking that there's some way, alone in your room, to solve for all the variables, anticipate solutions to those problems, and *then* you will sell.

It's like the dilemma I had with weight loss. What I *thought* was going to happen was I was going to lose weight, then I was going to be happy and think like a thin person. What *actually* had to happen was I had to be happy, think like a thin person, and then losing weight would even become *possible*. I'm not going to say it was super easy. When I was trying to eat less and exercise more, and I thought there was a day coming I would be happy. Every time I would get *unhappy*, what would I do? I would eat. You guys are doing the same thing. I hear this all the time. For instance, *I'm overwhelmed* or *I'm confused*. You believe you're overwhelmed. You have also learned that *I'm overwhelmed* is a sympathetic reason to stop.

I believed I was hungry, or at the very least, I believed that I couldn't resist the brownies. It turns out I can resist the brownies, and I also discovered I wasn't really that hungry. Actually, I just didn't want to fucking feel uncomfortable. Saying *I'm confused*, or saying *I'm overwhelmed*, announce choices that you are making to stay where you are. *Change* is uncomfortable. I really, really, really need you to know this part: I fully realize it doesn't feel that way from where you are on the journey right now. What I always say is, if there was any lie detector test in the land to ask me, "Do you want to be thin, or a normal healthy weight, not 100 pounds overweight?" I would have passed the lie detector test saying

I wanted to lose weight. I didn't realize I was *choosing* to stay overweight.

I promised if you're overwhelmed or confused, it's not because this stuff is overwhelming or confusing, it's that the alternative (which is *feeling uncomfortable*) is actually less pleasant to you than the safer alternative of choosing to feel overwhelmed or confused. You may be choosing it even if it doesn't feel that way, just like I was choosing to be overweight. I'm not accusing you of something here or suggesting you're weak and I'm strong. Let's be super clear. I lost 100 pounds or more, *five* fucking times. I did not learn all of what I teach by having things come easily, so there is no smug, blissful ignorance for what it takes to change, there is no denial of your experience and your feelings. The only reason I could teach this is I've been so fucking mad in it. It was torture.

You're going to think this is "too hard." That is just your brain trying to keep you where you are, because being confused is safer than growing. It does not get better in the pages of your journal with you endlessly trying to figure it out – you have to do the hard things. Just like your book can't make a difference to anyone while it stays in your head, your program can't make a difference from your head, either. We just have to get it out there and lead people to a place they can access it.

CHAPTER 3

"What's In It For Me" FM

It was freezing in the theatre. We got the space after hours. Rehearsals started at 11pm and would go until 1 or 2 in the morning, but it was also January in Washington DC. The temperature inside the theatre had to be in the low 60s, best case.

I sat in the middle of the audience and watched as the cast of the musical Baby sang and danced. As each one of them drew my focus, I would pop into their characters. I knew each character's back story intimately, why they were there, where they were going, what they wanted. And I knew what they would do.

As a director, I wanted the experience for my audience to be authentic — even if it was just a silly musical about having kids. When an actor would do something that I knew the character *wouldn't* do, I'd take a note.

I wanted to do work that legendary acting coach Sanford Meisner would appreciate. His standard is for the actor to "get out of their head" and to behave instinctively with the people and the environment the way a real person would. The character had to be a whole person on stage, not just a two-dimensional representation of a person.

Meisner was more interested in how people behaved rather than what they felt or said. (It's kind of the stage analog to Maya Angelou's teaching: "When people show you who they are, believe them.") Playing a feeling is really boring to watch but behaving truthfully in an imagined or created situation is captivating.

I got good at jumping in and out of the characters as they appeared on the stage, therefore knowing when the actor made a choice that was in their own head, versus when they were truly aligned with their role.

Years later, when I was ghostwriting books, I realized I was using those skills I'd learned as a theater director in college to get into character as the author who I was representing.
It wasn't me crafting the book, it was me, in character, as the author whose byline the finished book would feature.
I cast myself in the role of my employer and wrote from there. Somehow, when I wrote in character, my writing was faster, and the author who had hired me as a ghostwriter was happier.

I know this is not what Meisner intended to happen with his work, but what I realized is the skill of being able to get into character was essential to making my clients happy. When hiring a ghostwriter like me, the author still wanted the book to sound like them. Looking back now, I can see how this was a disservice to the reader, but it made my client happy!

You can make your clients happy with this technique, too.
If you can master this, it will make clients beg to work with you.

Most authors write what makes *them* happy, what they want to talk about, what they want to share. I call it an ego-fest. You can get a finished book this way, but it will not be a book that makes a difference, or gets clients banging down your door to hire you. This is because everyone has their personal radio dial tuned to "What's In It For Me" FM.

Your Ideal Reader

Now don't worry, I'm not going to have you doing scene work as part of this exercise, but I do want you to create a character you *could* play. And I call this character your "ideal reader." Now, your ideal reader isn't just anyone who could read and enjoy the book, your ideal reader is the person who finds the book by searching specifically to solve a burning and urgent problem, then reads the book in full on the day she gets it.

Before she even finishes reading it, she googles you and signs up for anything she can. By the time the book is read, she has already decided to hire you to work with her, and she has bought five more copies of the book to send to her friends because it has started to change her life. She signs up for your program within minutes of your first call and does everything you teach. Her results are amazing, and when you offer her the opportunity to continue working with you more intensively (or on her next problem), she doesn't hesitate. A couple of years later, she has spent $20,000 working with you, and she would spend more if she could. You have changed her life forever, and no amount of money invested could reflect the impact you have had on her.

Your ideal reader is one person who you *could* be cast to play in a story about her life. One person has a specific age, they are not in an age-range. Tune in to a specific name, a specific job, a specific house. And I want you to be able to describe whether there is dirt in the corner in her bathroom or not, because you know her so well. Remember, Meisner is interested in your ability to *behave* authentically in a given situation, and to do that you need to know everything about your ideal reader. Does her knee hurt? Does she have a tooth ache? Does she secretly have a favorite child?

The more you know about your ideal reader's back story, inner feelings and thought patterns, the more effectively you can project how she will authentically behave in a situation.

Get into Character

When you write your book, or any of the other marketing copy about your book, you want to read it back, in character, as your ideal reader.

I actually do a script analysis exercise I learned in a Meisner class. I take the manuscript, and for each line or paragraph, I write what my character is thinking and doing. When I do this, it's easy to see in my writing when I am instead in my own ego, excited to share something, but my ideal reader isn't ready to hear it.

If you take it back to weight loss, for instance.

There was a point in my life where I had lost 100 pounds, four times, on four diets: Weight Watchers, Jenny Craig, Nutrisystem and with a nutritionist. Diets work. I just couldn't keep the weight off. I found a book called *If I'm so Smart, Why Can't I Lose Weight?* by Brooke Castillo. In the book, what Brooke actually teaches is how to uncover hidden thought and belief systems that are leading you to overeat. But if she had said that, I would not have been interested in the book. Instead what she said was, *I know you're super smart, I know you've done everything right, so why hasn't it been working? Let me help you unlock the key. It's not that you've been doing the wrong stuff, it's just that you haven't had all the information.*

Of course, the information she helped me unlock was that I had poisonous belief systems that needed radical rewiring, but if she told me all that *before* I bought the book, I never would have bought it! I would not have accepted it, been interested in it, or believed her. I was still believing in my problem.

One of my clients was telling me about someone who tried to sell her new search engine optimization services for her website. The way the consultant tried to sell it was by telling her everything he observed that she'd done wrong with her website. Now, he didn't ask what she'd tried before, didn't ask how much money she'd spent on it, or even ask how important it was to her to get better search engine results. It turns out she had spent quite a lot of money as well as time and energy trying to get her search engine optimization right. Essentially the sales person was saying, "You're an idiot, you've done everything wrong, and you wasted a ton of money. Hire me."

You cannot make your client "wrong," and then ask for their money. It would just be an unnatural behavior for that person to hire you. You're invalidating their judgment, putting their belief in themselves into question so they already feel like an idiot, and now you're virtually calling them names and then asking them to spend money with you. Most people don't realize they're doing that, because they're talking in *their words*. In this guy's mind, he's just expressing what he's learned, i.e., "Everyone knows you have to put meta tags on the home page," or whatever tactical truth he's thinking.

It's delivery. If he had worded it more like, "I love what you're doing, and you got a lot of great stuff in place already. I see some really quick wins that we could get for you, I'd love to show you some simple and effective ways to make the SEO you already have in place pop." Now, all of a sudden, he's complimented her, and observes she *has the problem* which is, bluntly, the shit she's done isn't working. She's well aware of that. This time, he said it in an affirmative way where it's like, "you've done a bunch of stuff we can leverage. There's just a few little levers we can change." Even if there isn't much in common between his SEO solution and hers, he has framed it as though he sees her as competent and capable of integrating some upgrades, and *worth investing in.*

This is the magic of how your message will naturally shift when you can get into character as your ideal reader. It is *the* key to being able to make a difference and actually help people.

Your Testimonials Probably Suck

This is also why many of your testimonials aren't very helpful because your testimonials will say something like, "I learned what it was to love myself." Nobody's signing up and paying much money for loving themselves. They're signing up for answers, i.e., "How do I deal with my toxic boss?"

If all of your marketing is talking about "you're already good enough, nothing's wrong with you, and you don't have to change your toxic boss to be happy," you're going to have trouble selling your program because that's not what people are buying. If I were to write a testimonial for Brooke Castillo (the author of *If I'm So Smart, Why Can't I Lose Weight*) right now, I might be tempted to say something like, "I've realized the reason I was overweight for so long was because I wasn't willing to take accountability for my thoughts." That is the truth, and that insight is what was worth all the money I spent on integrating it, but that testimonial would not help her sell anything! What Brooke's *prospects* want is the result, so they want to hear me say, "When I started working with Brooke, I was over 315 pounds and hadn't looked at the scale in over a year because I was afraid of what the number would be. Today, I'm 167 pounds." That's also true. It's what they can relate to at the point they might purchase.

Your prospects need to know the result they can obtain, in terms they can actually hear, *before* they understand the real problem that is causing the symptoms or circumstances they want to change.

Don't Talk to Strangers

One of the things your wee portal needs is a latch. You need to have a way to *only* spend time and energy talking to people who have the problem you solve. You need to spare your energy and resources from the people who aren't likely to be a fit.

I recommend that you have an application process that helps qualify the people you will talk to, and at the same time, sets you up as the authority on the problem. You offer their dream come true, which is the results they have not yet achieved on their own. Here are the types of questions I recommend you ask on that application:

- Are you serious about getting the (dream come true)?
- How much longer are you willing to not have the
  (dream come true)?
- Why don't you have the (dream come true)?
- Why are you committed to working to get this (dream come true)?
- Are you looking for a coach to make sure you get your (dream come true)?

If they don't want the dream come true, what is the point of you spending time on the call with them?

If they *actually* want a different dream come true, even if they are not aware of that in themselves, you can learn to recognize those patterns. What they're going to tell you, go ahead and believe… their behavior will not lie. For instance, they're going to spend an hour with you, they're going to have a lovely chat with you. Then they need to ask their husband, or they need more time, they don't have the money right now. It doesn't mean they're asking their husband or they can't get the money right now, or that next week would be a better time to decide. It means *I either don't have that problem and that dream come true, I am not ready to do the work*, or *I don't believe you could get it for me*.

Remember to get clients begging to work with you, you want to limit your language to things that will make *your ideal reader* respond. If you tell them how you are going to solve the problem with them, you will see your ideal reader will lose interest. You want to focus on all the aspects of one problem and one dream come true, worded many different ways!

What it Takes

For your readers to beg to work with you, there are only two things that will matter:

1. The clarity of the wee portal – and the result you will help them achieve.
2. Your confidence in who you are, and that you are going to get them there.

If you know someone else who can do a better job to get them the result they want, then you should refer them to that person. If you do not know anyone else who can do a better job getting them that result, congratulations! You are the best in the world at solving this one problem for this person. *Claim that position!* I can tell you the best in the world never has to say, "I'm the best in the world." They just *are* that person, and their prospects can tell by their demonstrated results and their confidence.

This isn't being an impostor, or having a big ego, it's just the facts.

If you are confident that they're going to get a 10X return on their investment, that their life is going to be 10 times better, if they're a good fit for your program, that's what matters.

Don't Charge What you are Worth

Most of you assigned a dollar value to your hours, at some point, and you have no problem with this. You have no problem assuming you're worth $50 an hour or $100 an hour or $25 an hour, and your proof is probably that people pay you these rates. If somebody directed you, *Give me your hourly rate*, you might go back to your last job and do some quick math and say, "Well, I was making $60,000 a year which is roughly $30 an hour, but if this is on a contract, I'm going to charge $60 an hour." You could figure out your hourly rate backwards from experience. That's how most people choose what to charge. I don't want you to trade time for money anymore, though. I want you to trade results for money. Instead of having an hourly rate, I want you to have a value rate.

It is time to stop thinking like somebody whose time is worth money and start thinking like somebody who *creates results that are worth money*. I talk all the time about your best client should be able to easily get a 10X return on his or her investment.

A lot of you who don't have business coaching or experience directly related to it under your belts just heard, *I'm going to help you get a better job that pays 10 times as much* or something. You just gloss this over. I realized that the part most of my clients were missing is you're unsure about charging for your value, not your time.

What are you afraid of? What do you think you need to know in order to sell? To charge what your result is worth to your ideal client?

CHAPTER 4

They Can't Buy from You if They Don't Know Who You Are

In my favorite episode of the animated TV show, *South Park,* one of the characters has an idea to start a business selling underpants. In the show, they present the business plan. Here it is:

Step One - Collect Underpants
Step Two - ?
Step Three - Profit

Of course, this is funny because you can't simply go from collecting underpants to making a profit without something significant happening in between. *Awareness* is that missing link!

This is the entire part that matters. You can have the best product in the world, but if you don't have a way to *get people to find out about it*, raise their hands and say that they want to know more about that product, and then buy the product, you can't end up with any profit.

When you are writing a book, or creating a product, it *feels* like the important part is creating that thing you are going to sell. It seems like the important parts of the equation in this South Park business are collecting the underpants (in our case this would be writing the book) and then collecting the money. But there can be no collection of money unless there is someone, who wants to buy, to collect it from. In order to ever profit from creating or selling your product, people must become aware of you.

Never, in the history of human civilization, has someone bought something *before* they had heard of it. It's simple physics. You must know about something before you can buy it – even if only by seconds. Your job, as an author, whether you are self-published or have a six-figure advance from a traditional publisher, is also to make people aware of you and your book. Where most authors fall apart in this responsibility is doing that with consistency. Many authors try several different things when their book first comes out – a book signing, an online event, an ad or an article in a local paper – but when they don't see traction and momentum right away, they give up.

Author Dr. Joe Dispenza talks about this beautifully in the book *Breaking the Habit of Being Yourself.* Dr. Joe explains our brain's way of keeping us safe. It turns out that neurologically, from the processes by which our brains are developed, we become biologically wired to stick with the status quo. Every morning we wake up, notice we didn't die last night, and to our brains that means whatever happened yesterday was success, so it (unconsciously) processes, "We should do all that again because then we get to stay alive tomorrow." Your brain always wants you to stay safe, right where you are. It's been programmed to influence you that way biologically, because otherwise you could die.

To get awareness about your book, I might suggest you go speak once a week. But say you have never spoken with regularity before, so your brain is wondering subconsciously: "What happens if when you speak, you get shot, like Martin Luther King? *You could die!* My recommendation is you keep surfing Facebook and watching Netflix – that worked well yesterday. *You lived!*"

Your brain's whole job is to keep you alive. The things that I'm suggesting you do, to grow the momentum needed to fill your coaching business with clients begging to work with you, are probably new. They will make your subconscious mind fear these uncomfortable activities, even suspect they may kill you. The truth is, hiding doesn't always keep you safe. What's more, it's just not an effective strategy to make an impact.

That's why I'm going to ask you to make a critical and essential commitment right now, before you read another word of this book. In this chapter, I will share with you the ways you can effectively get the word out about your book. There will be many ideas in this chapter, and you might be feeling confused and overwhelmed. If you are going to read forward, however, I need you to commit *now* that you will pick a strategy to grow awareness about you and your book and stick to it for at least 90 days – with consistency – even if you feel like switching paths. The urge to switch is hard-coded into your brain in its survival mode, and the only way to route a new path into your brain is to consistently do something new, and slowly demonstrate to your brain its safety and results.

One you make the commitment to keep going, even when it gets hard or boring or frustrating, I want to stick to one awareness method to pursue. **With limited resources. it's impossible to fund and optimize multiple channel strategies at once.**

Pick one tool that you think is going to be most effective *for you*. What's going to be most effective is what you're already good at, so if you love speaking you should speak. If you love writing, you should write, and if you like being interviewed, you should be interviewed...for media, podcasts, or blogs, for instance. There's not a right or wrong way, except that whatever you pick *must feel good to you,* in part because it's more likely to work if you have done it before, and in part because if you don't like it you will probably quit – or at least want to, and that makes it harder to get results.

Top 10 Ways ACTUAL Authors Have Increased Awareness for Their Books

1. Live events
   a. Conferences
   b. Hosting conferences
   c. Trade shows
   d. Attending events
   e. Leading a large Meetup group

2. Speaking
   a. Speaking at every woman's group in the area for free.
   b. Speaking to parent groups.
   c. Speaking to business groups.
   d. In person communities that they already engage in and serve in.
   e. In person presentation, chamber of commerce or similar affinity group
3. Networking (Don't go in trying to sell to people. Build relationships.)
   a. BNI or other paid networking group
   b. The gas station
   c. The grocery store
   d. The parking lot
   e. Church
   f. Coffee shops (flyer)
   g. Vacations
   h. Auto Mechanics Shop
   i. Uber/Lyft Drivers
   j. Volunteering
   k. Coworking spaces
   l. Ski slopes

m. Yoga shalas

n. Vipassana retreats (after the meditation finished obviously!)

o. Surfing

4. Social Media

a. LinkedIn groups

b. Instagram commenting

c. Networking in Facebook groups

d. Daily Facebook Lives with interviews

5. Referrals

a. Local healing practitioners

b. Therapists

c. Naturopaths

d. Doctors

e. Business owners

f. Yoga teachers

g. Friends!

h. Family

i. Past clients

j. Former co-workers

k. Lawyers

6. Direct Mail

a. Sending letters to everyone in my kid's PTA handbook

b. Postcard mailers to my list from SendOutcard

c. Sending my book to CEO's trying to grow their business.

7. Media coverage

a. HARO (Help a Reporter Out)

b. Podcast Guest

8. Gig Boards

a. Craigslist

b. Upwork

c. Thumbtack.com

9. Collaborations

a. Spa days

b. Customer appreciation nights

c. Partnerships with other coaches

10. Writing

a. Articles for magazines

b. Guest blog post

Within each of these buckets of awareness activities, there are millions of different subtleties. There is a lot to learn to become the best in the world at getting people to know about you this way. So once you pick, you are going to focus on doing it for at least 10 hours a week (ideally you will invest 20 hours a week) for the next 90 days. Your goal is *not* to instantly get it right out of the gate. Your goal is to figure out how to become amazing at one method or channel for getting known, for making other people aware of your book and your work.

This list is not comprehensive. There are millions of options, and you can brainstorm a lot more of them specific to where you live, or the kind of work you do. Go through everything that you could possibly do, and then see what category your favorite things cluster in. Pick that one category that you are going to absolutely master. So that's step one: Identify one awareness activity, at a high level, that you are going to focus on for 90 days, becoming the world's best expert on your own behalf.

When I say, "get good at it," I mean that you need to develop your skill and execution in the tactics, and you need to develop the management insight to support it. A good awareness channel is an awareness channel that generates enough leads to fill your practice. The reason we need at least 120 hours of evidence (ideally more like 250 hours) is because we have to be able to demonstrate and measure what works, and what doesn't, for you in this channel. To have something to measure and repeat, we need to generate enough data for our conclusions from it to mean something. We need you to go to ten networking events, do your best to make connections, and see how many clients come from that, so we can measure the effectiveness of your ability to get clients from networking events. Or we need you to hand out 1000 flyers in front of a coffee shop and see how many people call you to inquire about services, and of those, how many become clients from that flyer.

You've got to actually do something and measure its success. When we know what's working, we can adjust it, or revise our approach altogether. We can decide if it was the networking events that were a bad fit, or maybe your skills, or your ability to identify a prospect among your attendees, may need refining.

Most Authors *think* they failed because they picked the wrong awareness tactic.

Most Authors *actually* fail because they don't do the work required to bring awareness to their work.

Authors who fail commonly fall into two categories when it comes to promoting their book:

1. They do little to nothing, spending less than an hour a week promoting their work.
2. They do a multitude of different things to promote their book, but they never get really good at developing an awareness method that leads to actual clients.

Authors who succeed:

1. Have a single, focused, clear and consistent way to bring awareness to their work.
2. Spend at least ten hours a week promoting themselves through that single channel.

Authors don't fail because they picked the wrong tactics, they fail because they quit, or are too scattered or tentative. This is because they have failed to do the internal energetic work required to get your brain to settle down, and relax, for the fact is that you will not die if you do something different.

The Difference Between Good Failure and Bad Failure

There are so many conflicting messages aimed at people who are building a business. They tell you to trust your gut, and then they *also* tell you the good stuff happens outside your comfort zone. They tell you to "fail fast," but then they *also* say take "aligned" action. I think the number one thing an entrepreneur can do to succeed is learn to discern between the contrasting, but equally correct, messages they will receive.

The reason I want you to commit to your awareness plan for 90 days is so that we get enough data to make smart decisions. That said, if you pick a plan that makes you want to jump off a bridge, you might change your method and restart the timer. Your job is to discern if making that change is actually an excuse, or an avoidance path, instead of a choice in service of your business. No one can do that work for you, and really, having a coach is the only way I have found to help me see into those blind spots.

To me, there are two kinds of failure. There is failure created by not taking action because you are "trying to figure things out," "waiting for the right time," or "needing to be in alignment." And there is failure created by taking action and not getting the desired results. The second type of failure here is *good* failure – the kind that people mean when they say "fail fast." Bad failure is thinking about it as merely *possible* action, but not pushing forward into acting at all. Good failure is trying things that may or may not lead to clients and doing some of them badly – but even those failures are meaningful. Your tactic either works and gets leads or works because it gets the information you need to know to improve. You can never get the insight, feedback, or confidence you need from sitting back and trying to figure it all out before you do anything.

CHAPTER 5

Live It to Give It

I looked out over a crowd of 3,000 people at the Sony Center in Toronto and took a breath. I had fifteen minutes to inspire the right people in the audience to get a free copy of my book, *Make 'Em Beg to Publish Your Book.* The audience was filled with mission-driven entrepreneurs, and I knew from some pre-event research that over 60% of attendees said they wanted to write a book. This was, for me anyway, a room of hot prospects.

As you will remember from Chapter 4, speaking at an event where your prospects already are gathered is a great way to get awareness about your book. Sometimes, these engagements will be available to you as an author at no cost. Other times, you might decide to make an investment. For me, at this event, each minute I was on the stage was costing me close to $2,500. I had to be good.

Before I left the stage, 450 audience members had downloaded my ebook. It actually cost me $77 for each book I gave away!

Most people who write a book think about how they are going to make $10 or $15 a book. I am asking you to turn this assumption on its head. I know one of the secrets to writing a book that makes clients beg to work with you is budgeting how much *you* will *spend* to get each book in your prospect's hands.

And here is where the math gets interesting. Of the 450 folks who got my book, 42 of them signed up to learn more about working with me, and 11 of those decided it was the right time for them to invest in getting their book done. Those 11 clients generated $343,750 in revenue for me over the following year by making further investments with me to reach their goals.

My $35K investment (plus the cost of the books) generated a nearly 10 to 1 return because I was willing to lead with my book. Giving away your book as a *magnet* for *leads* (known as a lead magnet) is the single most effective marketing strategy for getting clients who want to work with you.

Just by the fact that you have written and published a book about the problem, the person opting in to get the book has an indication that you are:

1. An expert on the topic
2. A serious business person
3. Committed to your work
4. Not flakey

This alone goes a huge way to differentiating you from the others that they might hire.

But there is *still more* a book does as a lead magnet… in that giving it away is magnanimous. Giving it away is generous and kind, and it just feels so great doing it (which inspires positive feeling, which is itself attractive). One of the reasons why a free book is one of the best lead magnets of all time in history is because it has inherent perceived value. Even if you give away the ebook, the moment you're offering it, people see your book is worth roughly ten to twenty dollars. It's kind of like the number in their head that a book has to cost, so it has a value. This is a generous way to start a relationship. There is no other lead magnet with this level of concrete perceived value.

This is why, if you want to write a book that gets clients begging to work with you, you are going to need to drop the idea of your book as a source of revenue. Period. A book that gets clients is not a product that generates income. Instead, it's a marketing tool that helps people self-select you as their coach or consultant. A book is a cost-center, not a revenue-center, for your business.

Know How Many Leads You Need

In order to budget how many books you will need to give away, you first need to know how many clients makes a full practice for you. My clients, when starting out, typically need to give away 100 books to get a client. Let's use my example from that speech. I gave away 450 books, and I got 11 clients. That was 1 client for every 41 books I gave away. But I wasn't hitting numbers like that out of the gate. Because I have narrowly focused my awareness techniques, and I target the right audience to speak to (the one who has 60% of their members thinking about writing a book), I have been able to improve my numbers.

Let's say you want to have 10 clients a month. You will need to plan on giving away at least 100 books. Of those 100 people, 20 to 40 might inquire about working with you. Depending on how good your sales skills are (we'll cover that later in the book) you will likely be able to close somewhere between half and a quarter of those inquiries.

Now you should be asking, *How can I give away 100 books a month to highly qualified prospects?* If you can do that, it's inevitable that you will get your clients. The answer to that question is picking the *right* awareness method for you and optimizing the hell out of it.

Your awareness efforts have to match up with the number of books you need to give away.

Your Book Doesn't Need to Be Finished to Give It Away

The great news is you don't have to wait until your book is completed to find out how effective this strategy is. You don't need to have written a book at all (yet) to use it as a lead magnet. You can say *I'm writing a new book about (whatever your book is about), if you would like to sign up for an early copy of the new book, I will send it to you as soon as it's done, as a way of saying thank you.*

Let's say your new book is all of the reasons why you should buy a new bicycle. When you are speaking, or networking, or doing whatever you do for awareness, you just say, "I'm writing a new book about how to buy the perfect bicycle, and if you want to sign up for a free copy of this book…. (and figure out how you take those orders)."

When I was writing this book, I posted this message on Facebook just after I completed my first chapter:

"My next book, MAKE 'EM BEG TO BE YOUR CLIENT is happening.

I'm finally writing the book so many people have begged me for. This is going to be the definitive guide to writing a book that fills your coaching practice. Glad to be writing this one with my friend, client and ideal reader in the room next door. Perfect inspiration and motivation to finish by sunset tomorrow!

If you already have a book and it's not getting you clients like you hoped (or if you want to write a book that gets clients begging to work with you), sign up to be an early reader. Let me know in the comments and I'll get you a copy before I make it publicly available."

That gets them to raise their hand, while simultaneously giving it a perceived value. It's going to be a book. It's really that simple! Now if someone raises their hand and says, "Yes! I want to write a book that gets clients begging to work with me." Then, I know I can invite them to work with me right now.

I can reply to each person and say: "Great! Thanks for your interest in writing a book that gets clients begging to work with you. My book is going to be out really soon, and I will send it to you, but I don't want you to have to wait. I'd love to jump on the phone right now." This is when you are most likely to convert a sale because your prospect is thinking, *Man, I have to solve this problem!*

Every day that passes the chance of them becoming a client decreases. Yes, give them the book whenever it's ready. If it's ready in two months, if it's ready four months, give them the book. You made a promise so fulfill the promise 100%, even if time has passed. Remember, the real purpose of the lead magnet is not to give them the book. The purpose of the lead magnet is to get them to raise their hand and say, *I have this problem,* the minute they realize they have the problem that your work solves.

Make it Personal

The way to give your book away is to *only* talk about the problem your book solves, and the *result* readers get from implementing the solutions in the book. Never discuss the how or the details of the solution itself when you are offering the book. You just want to focus on the problem, and how you hold the key to their dream come true.

How you're going to deliver the book to them? Well, you can store a PDF on a cloud storage system, and just email the link to them – or you can print it out.

Of course, you can also create a beautiful web page where people get your book, but you honestly don't have to. Personal emails work just fine!

I frequently participate in Facebook groups. When somebody asks a question that shows they might be a prospect for me, I offer to give them a copy of my book. Emailing a copy of my book (with an offer to talk to me on the phone) in this way has helped me to generate hundreds of thousands of dollars of business. If your awareness method is participating in social media, then this is all you need to have ready to go in order to generate enough qualified leads that you can fill your practice.

Give A Book Away PLUS

There is no one way to do a free book offer. One of my favorite methods is to run ads to promote them. I've also done it with an eCourse (you can see the eCourse in The Author Incubator's YouTube Channel). When someone signed up for the book, it came with a companion class. This is a great way to give a ton of value away early in the relationship, and to overcome the problem of people not actually reading your book after they get it.

Just Pay Shipping

You can also give away a printed book, and you can charge just for the shipping, if you want to. As a self-published author, I spend about $3 per printed copy of my books. To ship domestically is another $3. You can offer to give your $15 book away for free, in exchange for someone paying $3 - $6 for shipping. Very often the "free, just pay shipping" offer actually covers the author's full costs. You will give away fewer books this way, but the people who are willing to pay anything to get your book, even a heavily discounted price, will be more committed and convert at a higher rate to becoming clients.

Clickfunnel's CEO, Russell Brunson, gave away something like 80,000 copies of his book in just 30 days. Because the recipients paid for shipping, he was also able to make other, add-on offers after people committed to getting the book. In this way, he generated thousands of clients. I don't like to ask for a sale at the same time I'm giving my book away, but I do like to send and receive paper copies of books, so this is a great way to get an interested an engaged lead.

If you are going to do print book give-aways though, you will need a way to collect payment online, and it can get messy. Make sure you give away lots of free ebooks before you go this path.

There is no right or wrong way to give your book away. I have seen it done dozens of different ways and they can all work, as long as you remember the one cardinal rule of using a book as a lead magnet: The minimum cost of the book is the prospect's *contact information*.

Give your book away to people who choose to *opt in*, that is *raise their hand*, acknowledging they have the problem your book solves. Make sure you get their *contact information and* follow up with them. If they are ready to fix the problem, you are the most likely one to help them do just that!

CHAPTER 6

Serve. Don't Chase.

"A lot of would-be founders believe that startups either take off or don't. You build something, make it available, and if you've made a better mousetrap, people beat a path to your door as promised. Or they don't, in which case the market must not exist. Actually, startups take off because the founders MAKE them take off... The most common unscalable thing founders have to do at the start is to recruit users manually. Nearly all startups have to. You can't wait for users to come to you. You have to go out and get them."

– Paul Graham, Y Combinator

This book is all about writing a book that gets clients begging to work with you. But at the very beginning, how do you rectify that with the need to go out and manually recruit users before you have visibility or momentum? It can feel like a catch-22.

My client Margo came to me in a bit of a money crunch. She had already quit her full-time job in project management because it was "sucking her soul dry," six months before she signed up to write a book with The Author Incubator. Her savings were dwindling, but she knew she needed to invest in herself to grow her business, so she took a line of credit and made a promise to her husband. "I'm going to do this," she told him, "but I will have that credit line paid down in 90 days."

One of the things I teach my authors is to start selling their services right away, if they aren't already, so she knew she was going to have to put an offer out there soon, to get her investment back.

Margo was worried because she hadn't had consulting clients before. She wanted to take her project management experience from the defense contractor she worked at and apply it to help local businesses in her area improve their productivity. The company she worked for was running on Six Sigma, and her new clients were running mostly on blood, sweat and tears. She knew there was an easier way, and she wanted to share it with them.

"Angela," she said to me, "I just don't get it. You say the prize never chases, but then you tell me to go knocking on the doors of local businesses in my town. That just feels really…. *chasey*!"

Margo was right. There is a natural dichotomy between the energy of hustling and the energy of laying back while you've primed your customers to beg you to work with them. But there doesn't have to be, if you understand the process of searching for hand-raisers.

Most people go out looking for new business thinking thoughts like Margo had: "I promised my husband I'd get this debt paid down. I really hope this person decides to buy from me." This is *not* an attractive energy, and it will not generally lead to clients. When it *does* lead to clients, it leads to non-ideal, challenging clients – ones who are seldom satisfied.

To find customers who are extremely likely to be satisfied, you have to get them to invite *you* to be their coach or consultant. Your job isn't to convince *them* to buy anything from you. Your job is to help them get *clarity* on the gap between where they are now, and where they want to be. Then, if they see you as the person who can get them to where they want to be, they will, quite literally, beg you to accept them as a client. (By the way, whether you do accept them or not is really up to you. I accept fewer than 20% of people who ask to work with me, and I only accept the people I know will get amazing results.)

When you are giving away your book (as we reviewed in the last chapter), you are getting people to raise their hand to say, "Yes! I have the problem you wrote this book about. YES! I want to solve it." Now we don't know for sure if they actually *do* have that problem and we really don't know if they want to *solve* it. That's going to take more exploration together, but we have a breadcrumb that indicates they might.

The problem is, if someone buys your book, or gets it from a friend, you have no way of knowing how to reach them to explore those desires. In addition to having a book as a lead magnet, every author needs a *secondary* lead magnet. I call it a Reader Magnet. This is the lead magnet that only goes inside your book.

Good vs. Bad Lead Magnets

Great ideas for lead magnets have some things in common – essentially, they prepare a reader to buy from you.

A reader magnet can be repurposed even if people haven't read the book, and they help the reader diagnose the *actual* problem they need to invest in fixing.

Terrible ideas also have some things in common: they make a reader feel like their problem is solved already when it's not. They give the reader a false sense of resolution and comfort. They make it easier for the reader to procrastinate about doing the work, and really solving the problem.

Books, especially those written using the Difference Process™ that I outline in my first book, The Difference, are great lead magnets. But you can't give your book away again in your book. With your reader magnet, you want to ask yourself these three questions to determine if your lead magnet is effective:

1. Does it give a sense of instant completion rather than creating more work or put something on your to do list?
2. Can you use it as a lead magnet independently of the book?
3. Does it help the reader diagnose the problem they need to invest in fixing?

Your Book Needs a Companion Webinar

The most effective lead magnet, besides a book, is a webinar. The word webinar means lots of things to lots of people. I'm not even sure what it means. It could just be a large group phone call. It could include a slide presentation with a voice-over. It could be a video presentation that doesn't have any slides or images. For purposes of this conversation, it actually doesn't matter how you present the information – video, audio, slides, live or recorded – but it does matter how you structure the presentation and share it. And it doesn't matter what you call it, either: a webinar, a presentation, a companion class… you choose what feels yummy and appealing to your ideal reader. For this book, I'm calling it a webinar.

In fact, at the beginning, I want you to do these in whatever way is easiest for you and which requires the least cost and time. I want to get you used to doing this in a small amount of time, even if you have nothing else going on.

Let's say you have no kids, you have no self-care needs, you have no sleep needs, you are happy to spend 100 hours this week on it, I still want you only spending four hours to get this tactic done, so you will learn what that pace feels like. Here's the news flash: If you've got perfectionism issues, this is where you get to drop them all, because there's no way to do this perfectly in four hours. In fact, if you spend 400 hours on it, there is also no way to do it perfectly. There's a way to get it done and to get some data, but there's not a way to do it perfectly, so we just got to give that idea right up. Perfection, I mean competence, can only come from doing it – and maybe even doing it badly a bunch of times. This is more of the *good* kind of failing I referenced earlier in the book.

When I started off, I did webinars weekly. There were no slides, no video, I just used a free conference call phone line! Most weeks, there were only a handful of people on the calls. Almost every week, one of those attendees would become a client.

Start with Your Numbers

Let's start with your numbers. Your very first task to get clients begging to work with you is to know your numbers, why? Because you are the CEO, and as the CEO you are responsible for your business.

I can't know them for you and I can't give it to you. This seems like some extra thing, you might be thinking in your head right now, "I just want as many as I can get." As many as I can get means zero. That does not work. You have probably tried that strategy. It's ineffective. Let's not do something we've already proven month after month does that not work. We want to have a specific number.

Your goal is to know what we need to do this week. I recommend that a full practice for a coaching business takes between one and five clients a week. You can easily have a 20-hour a week, $10K a month, six-figure business starting with one new client a week. If you want a $100K a month, seven-figure business, you will be looking at more like five new clients a week, and probably a few employees to help you out.

Think about how many clients do you really need to get each week. If you are, let's say, trying to get two new clients a week, you will need to get about 20 people on the webinar to hit that goal but since it will be free, it's likely less than 50% of people who register will actually attend. I usually see webinar attendance rates of 20% - 40%, so you will need something like 50 people to *register* for the webinar to get 20 people to *show up*, and two of them will go on to become clients.

Do THIS. Not THAT.

When starting out, what you likely want to start with, which by the way, we've already established doesn't work, is what's in the webinar or what is the title of the webinar.

Wrong place to start.

We know that doesn't work. You've tried that. Let's not go there again. The reason I don't start with what the content is, and I start with what my numbers are instead, is because it's not the tactics that determines success or failure, it's really the ownership and the thinking.

My topic, my title, my content, all might change depending on my numbers. If I want to do something that I know I don't have a list for, or my list isn't interested in it, I'm going to have to have a different hook to get people in. The order that I'm teaching this in is very systemized.

I want you to start with your numbers because that's going to help you think about what you can create and what you can get people actually to raise their hand and say, "Yes, I have that problem."

How Do I Get People To Come?

I recommend you regularly promote your free book and your free webinar. Don't chase for sales. Instead, use these two free tools to serve deeply. This book is not a technical guide to setting up registration pages, so I'm going to assume you have some technology in place, web skills, or can get them on board. But here are a few tips that might help, so when you are sending people you meet in your awareness activities to sign up for your webinar, you have a place to send them.

Ways people can give you their contact information in exchange for a "ticket" to your webinar:

- Create a Facebook group or event for the webinar.
- Create a simple landing page with a tool like Square Space or Lead Pages.
- Use Eventbrite and make free tickets available.
- Upload your webinar into an automated webinar system like Stealth Seminars or Evergreen Business Systems and use their landing page tools.
- Put up a blog post and integrate the email collection form from your mail host on that page.

Remember, you have a goal for the number of registrants you need so make sure when you are doing awareness, you are sending people who hear about you to a registration page with great marketing content, so they still want to be part of what you are doing. Make sure the only way they can come to your webinar is if they "pay" with their email address.

Collaborate!

Another great way to get people to sign up for your webinar is through friends and colleagues.

Two of my clients, Jeanne Andrus, the menopause guru, and Jill Angie, of Not Your Average Runner, make a great example of how to do this well. Jeanne believes that many of her menopause clients should run. Jill has many running clients who are going through menopause or pre-menopause. They are not competitive in their work, but at the same time, their work is very complementary. Who do you know well who has a business that yours may complement?

Can you offer to do a webinar for people
they invite?

What Do I Say?

Once all of that is done, then, and only then, can
you ask yourself the question, "What the heck
am I going to talk about in this thing?"

I like to think of your presentation in thirds. And
remember the *goal* of the presentation is not to
get them to buy anything – not at all. The goal
is to get them to see the gap between where
they are and where they want to be. Once that is
determined, they will know if they want you to
help them close that gap.

In the first third of your presentation, the goal
is to make it abundantly clear to the viewer or
listener that you deeply understand the problem
they are facing and that you know the value in
solving this problem. In this section, you will
want to share case studies of how you came to
solve this problem for yourself and for a couple
of your clients. Most people start with their bio.

This is a terrible way to start because nobody really cares about your bio. If they are giving you an hour of their time, it's because they care about themselves, and are exploring whether or not they want to solve this problem.

You might be wondering, "Why will they listen to me if I don't give them my bio?" Because they already raised their hand and said they want to hear. You can include your bio but include it at least 10 minutes in after you have made it very clear you deeply understand the pain associated with the problem you solve.

In the next third of your presentation, you want to give practical, tangible, concrete advice. Very often these are steps or tips. It could be three secrets that people need to know, or the three most common mistakes that people make. This is the meat of the presentation. This gives them a sense of whether you truly solve the problem and previews what it would be like to work with you.

The final third of your presentation is the *close*. Remember we aren't closing them on the *sale* itself. we are closing them on clarity about whether or not they want to take the next step in closing the gap between where they are and where they want to be. Here is where you share the challenges to solving this on your own without help. No lying, nothing fancy, no neuro-linguistic programming. We're not trying to trick anyone. You are an expert on this topic, so kindly share what happens when you try to close this gap on your own. This should be what you have already seen with your clients, or in your own life. This is another place to be heavily story-driven. And when you share stories, make sure you reference your clients, even without identifying information, so your reader knows they could hire you as well.

Finally, you're going to have a call to action. The call to action for almost everyone is some version of, "Now that you know the problem, the dream come true, and the steps, do you want to do it on your own — or do you want to do it with me? If you want to do it with me, let's hop on a call and talk about it."

I don't really recommend doing Q&A on the webinars. People will want it, and you will want to do it, but what I recommend is to skip it. It's a disaster if you get somebody who goes off the rails. What I do, because this is actually true for me, is as part of my close, I say: "I know a bunch of you are going to have questions and I want to answer them, but I want to respect everyone's time. I know a lot of your questions are going to be very personal, so what I'd love to do is just hop on the call with you, a private call with you, hear what's going on, and see if I can help."

It Works if You Work It

Work your awareness to get webinar registrations and don't stop until you get the number of people registered that is the goal for this week. Massive action is the key to success.

My last note for this step is that I want you to go into this first week with my definition of success or failure. Your definition of success or failure is probably, "Do I get lots of people to sign up and say I'm awesome?"

My definition of success or failure, which you should borrow this for this week is, *just doing it*. That's it. Right now, someone you could help is suffering. Sitting on your couch trying to figure it out will not help this person.

One of my first webinars, my Free Conference Call was a disaster. Why? I don't know, it broke, went down, like 15 minutes through the call, hung up. I lost everyone. You know what I did? I sent out an apology email and I re-did it the next day. No children were harmed. It was fine.

Is shit going to go wrong? For sure. Decide that in advance. Lots of shit is going to go wrong, you're going to screw it up, and you're going to do it anyway. By the way, if you do a ton of planning, you know what happens? Even more shit goes wrong, and it's more expensive. You cannot stop life from happening. You have to be the person who does it anyway.

Failing is having the technology crash.

Not failing is thinking about it and trying to solve the variables so you don't have that problem. That doesn't count.

When people say, fail fast, they mean go do something and have it actually break. They don't mean fail by sitting on your couch thinking about it.

Massive action is being 100% committed to having 20 people on your webinar this week.

Passive action is reading this chapter and thinking about it, preparing and never actually *doing* shit.

With passive action, you can never actually fail that, and that's why people choose it. The work is always "in progress," but it never gets to helping anyone.

When you keep consuming content, you keep growing. Go for it. It's super safe and cozy, but it isn't helping you help anyone.

You got to put shit out there and fail by doing a webinar that nobody comes to, in order that you can learn to do webinars that people *do* come to. It's fine. Your stuff doesn't have to be beautiful to help people.

You have a servant's heart, and an awareness that when we do new things, we are going to suck at them. Your clients are going to suck at the new things they try, at first. You need to model this ability to change and do imperfect, amateur things at the outset in order that you can grow, get better, and become the person who has the success. Who gets the results and gets out of her own way to get them. This is what your clients need from you. Not just what is in your head, but what is in your action.

CHAPTER 7

The L.O.V.E. Method of Sales

One of the most talented teachers I've had the pleasure of working with to write her book is named Theosophia Rose. Theosophia is a natural healer. When she looks in your eyes, you can actually physically feel your heart light up like a Christmas tree. And a hug from her is like a magical life force battery charge. Theosophia is soft spoken and unassuming. If you saw her at the Motor Vehicle Department, you would never guess she was actually a magical being. She operates Theosophia's Wisdom School, which is a training ground for seekers and spirit guides.

She was earning a living wage doing her work, but knew she was meant to reach more people so her work could serve an even greater purpose. And honestly, so did I.

I asked her how she sold people into her program, and she said she would get on a call and talk to people if they were interested. I asked her of all the people she talked to, how many signed up to work with her.

"Oh, I don't know, I guess just about all of them," she said in her understated way.

Just about all of them? What? Who closes 100% of prospects? Can you imagine what it would be like to be a sales person at a car dealership where you closed 100% of shoppers who walked through the door? Or to be a real estate agent who signed every home seller they met? In the world, 100% close rates are few and far between. And for good reason.

Maybe you heard that story and thought, *Wow! I need to see if Theosophia will help me close more sales.* It's easy to be envious of numbers like that, but there is a lie in those numbers. If you are closing 100% of offers you make, or even 50% of offers you make, and you aren't hitting your monthly revenue goals, or making the difference you want, and reaching the number of people you want to reach, you aren't making enough offers!

Get More Nos

I'm going to let you in on a big secret in the world of coaching and consulting. The reason most people don't have as much business as they want is because they simply don't make enough offers. My message to Theosophia, and to you, is to make more offers and get more nos.

How do you make more offers without chasing prospects down and sounding like a slimy sales person? Well, you make them come to you, of course!

Fresh blood is the life blood of business. A lot of people talk about building a list, but I have found a list is really a holding place for non-buy-

ers. Your list is where your leads go to die.
The *best* prospects to work with you are the ones who newly identified this problem in their lives and are 100% committed to solving it.

Imagine overnight your car was parked on the street, hit and run by someone, and demolished. You now have no car, a 30-minute commute to work, and a big ass problem. How long will you go without buying a car? Even if you don't have money saved… even if the insurance won't cover the full value of the car that was destroyed… even if you have other credit card debt you wanted to pay down first.

What are the chance you will just go without a car, join some marketing email lists from a few car dealerships, and wait for the right car or for inspiration to strike? How long will you sit on your couch and try to "figure out" the right car to buy? Are you willing to lose your job? Or risk damaging a car you borrowed? Or overpay for a rental car?

Maybe you will borrow a car for a little while or rent one. But I bet you will replace your car within 30 days.

Now I want you to imagine the person who would wait for 3, or 6, or 12 months to get a car. This person is now jobless, they are still, months later, complaining about the driver who hit him, suing the city for not having cameras on the street, and generally declining in health and vitality.

Is this the type of client you would want?

When you add people to your list and hope they will buy some day in the future, you are *hoping* for *terrible clients*.

The people on your email list who don't buy from you within 30 days either don't have the problem you solve, they don't want to solve it, or they have found someone else to solve it.

A Holding Place for Non-Buyers

Over a decade ago, I was diagnosed with something called Polycystic Ovarian Syndrome (PCOS). I came home from the doctor's office devastated my diagnosis would make it impossible for me to get pregnant. Immediately, I got on every PCOS and fertility mailing list I could find. Not long after, I found out I was pregnant! It was a miracle. I still had PCOS, but I got lucky. After I had my son, I made a major effort to get healthy and lost over 100 lbs. My PCOS went away, and I was "cured." But you know what? I'm still on most of those mailing lists. And I'm never going to buy!

The way to get clients begging to work with you is to consistently make new people aware of who you are and what problem you solve. Clients who will beg to work with you are in urgent need of solving this problem as quickly as possible. They *need* to get pregnant. They *need* a new car. They *need* you, now! If they don't need you now, they aren't going to beg to work with you. That's the first thing you need to keep in mind.

In order to consistently make new people aware of who you are, and what problem you solve, you still must spend a minimum of 10 hours a week making new people aware of you. Once they are aware of you, offer to serve them with your free book or your free webinar. If they are not willing to give you their contact information in exchange for that free service, they aren't going to beg to work with you. Don't worry about them.

If they do opt in for more free information from your book or class, they are raising their hand to say they have the problem you solve.

Don't sell anything. Just listen and love.

I want you to imagine someone standing in front of you, looking you in the eye and saying: "I have the problem you help people solve. Will you help me?" Would you turn away from them and walk the other direction? I bet you wouldn't. And yet, that's what *most* coaches actually do at this point.

Someone opts in to their lead magnet, and the coach just ghosts on them.

What?

My biggest, deepest, most frequent marketing advice to my authors is this…

The best way to get clients to beg to work with you is to LOVE THEM.

I tell my clients to imagine each person who downloads their book or registers for their webinar as a whole person. A person with a cranky spouse, a banged-up baby toe, a weird uncle in prison, a boss who sexually harassed them, an ex-boyfriend who still sends them weird messages on Facebook – just a whole actual perfectly, imperfect human. Then, to treat that person like a person. Just love them as a fellow human. Be interested in them and curious. Don't look at them with big dollar signs in their eyes. They aren't a transaction, they are a person. And you can love this person without ever making them an offer.

The reason Theosophia basically closed all of her sales calls was because she saw each person in 3D. The reason she didn't have as big of a platform as she wanted was because she wasn't talking to enough people.

Many marketing experts will tell you about building a big list and sending them tons of pre-written emails. I say no to all of that.

It's one thing if you are trying to sell lots of things to lots of people, but as a coach or a consultant, you just can't do a good job and get good results selling lots of things to lots of people.

The maximum number of clients I've seen a coach or consultant take on successfully is about 20 a month. Most of my authors start with the goal of bringing on just one or two new clients a week. To get one new client a week you need four people to request to talk to you. And to get four people to request to talk to you, you don't need tons of fancy automated email funnels and websites. You need email, or some sort of messaging tool, and you need to coach, care about, and get to know probably a dozen or two people each week. If you are sending a few personal, love-filled emails a day to hand-raisers who have opted into your lead magnet, you will end up with four or five requests for conversations, and one of those will make an offer.

But those conversations with the right people can't happen, unless you are still doing the awareness activities that will allow you to regularly and frequently give away your book and your webinar. If you aren't, then having more conversations won't help, because you will be talking to people who aren't urgently in need of solving a problem. You will end up trying to convince them why what you are selling is great, instead of looking them in the eye, listening to their problem, and, if you can help, offering to help.

To prepare for our sales call, it is your responsibility to remember this person with this problem has a whole life. I use an acting technique to really imagine them in their fullness as a human before the call. Sometimes use a candle, or a crystal, or an essential oil to help get grounded and remember there is nothing to sell but only love between humans to be shared. My personal belief is that while we are all individuals with free will, at the same time we are waves on the ocean, deeply connected and truly one. If I show up to a sales conversation WANTING to influence their free will or WANTING them to buy from me, I am dishonoring myself. It's my job to stay as clean and pure from wanting an outcome as possible. I don't know a lot about Buddhism but this is my rudimentary understanding of the concept of detachment with compassion.

I believe our job is sales is to stay 100% committed to relieving suffering, while staying equally committed to nonattachment and non-grasping. It's not my job to know what serves humanity at the highest and best, it's my job to be a channel for that to come through me whatever it looks like.

Introducing the L.O.V.E. Sales Method

Part 1: Let 'em Know They're Safe

Once your lead has expressed, through additional conversation, that they really do want to solve the problem and they would like to know more about what working with you to solve the problem might look like, I find the most effective approach is to get on a phone call with them. Doesn't matter if it's a video call or just voice, but I would schedule a full hour to really get to know them and discern if it would be a good fit to work together.

Think of this like running a corporate meeting. You need to set the tone and be in control. This isn't a democracy, it's not a conversation between two equals. You are the leader. You are the authority. You are the author. You are the person who has the solution to their problem. They may not want the solution to your problem in the end, but you are the person who has that solution, so you have to run the call.

If you make it seem like, "Hey, I want to talk to you about some ideas for what we could do together," and they get to give their ideas, and you get to give their ideas, and together you're going to collaborate on a solution, you're really not putting them in a position to succeed. They've already proven they can't solve this problem. They would not be on the call if they could solve this problem. If they have come so far as to show up on the call, you owe it to them to show up as the person who is already their coach. Their coach has to have the solutions for them.

If I said to our prospects, "How do you think we should write your book? Let's talk about what ways you work best." That tells you, "I don't know how to do this. I'm hoping you do."

Limit your small talk at the beginning, as you aren't there to be their friend, you are there to see if you can help them solve their problem.

I recommend you start the sales call with a question of, "Why do you want to invest your time today to solve this problem?" You want to remind them that their goal today is to focus on solving this problem.

Once you get that answer, you want to really kick off the call by setting the agenda. Here's what I say:

Okay, here's how today's call will work. First, I'm going to ask you a bunch of questions so I can find out more about you and what you're trying to accomplish. Then, I'll tell you what I've got going on over here, and you can ask me any questions that you want. Then, we'll decide if it's a fit to work together. Does that make sense?"

The three parts of that agenda are very important, the first thing is, I'm going to start. I'm in charge. I get to ask you questions. You're going to get them to agree to this. You're not being an asshole, but they're getting an hour of your time, this is how we do it.

You wouldn't go in to a doctor's office and expect them to tell you like, "Hey, can you use that stethoscope? I really think you need this one to check my ear." The doctor's like, "Here's how it's going to work. First, I'm going to do a physical examination. Then, I'm going to ask you some questions. Then, you can ask me any questions. Then, I'll give you the diagnosis and we'll decide what the next steps are."

You have to be that doctor. This cannot go out of order. The first thing is, "I get to ask you questions. I'm the doctor, I'm doing a diagnosis."

Now, the second part, there is a bit of a trick to. I don't use many tricks. I don't like anything where we're trying to trick people, but there is a trick here and you have to understand it. What I say to set the agenda is, "Then, I'll let you know what I've got going on over here." There is a trick to that sentence, here is what the trick is: I don't know if I want to sell you anything. I leave myself an out.

Remember I said, you aren't necessarily going to offer your services to everyone you get on a call with? In my case, I can only make offers to a small percentage of people. I don't want to lie when I set the agenda, so I don't say, "Then, I will describe my program to you." I say, "Then, I'll let you know what I've got going on over here." Because I might share to them about, I don't know, some free webinar I have coming up. I might share with them that I would love to give them a free copy of my book, especially the one they haven't yet read and seems to fit. I might share with them many other things that may not be my program. If I make a promise at the beginning, "Then, I will tell you about my program," I now need to either be a liar, or tell them about my program. I'm not willing to be a liar, so I have to tell them about my program. But I may not want to, because by the end of the call I've decided they may be not somebody I want to work with in that way.

This is the key to success on a sales call. It is not how you do the close, it's not about how many bonuses you throw in, it is how you set yourself up as alpha. If you promise them you will tell them about your program, then you've got to tell them about your program, and you've already lost the sale. I only tell people about my program if they are a fit for my program. I love and respect my prospects enough to not tell them about stuff that is not a good fit for them.

The third piece of this teeny tiny paragraph I start the sales call with is: "Then, we'll decide if it's a fit." The prospect thinks the goal is to get information and go think about it, but I know the purpose of this call is to make a decision as to whether they are going to solve this problem. I get them to agree to that from the start.

Ninety-nine percent of the time at this point, they say, "Sounds great." By the way, if they say anything than other than "sounds great," get off the fucking phone. It's a trap. Bad, bad, bad news. If they're like, "Actually, I just wanted to know how much your program costs, first." "Fantastic. Thank you so much for asking. Here's what I know, if you need to start with that question, I know we're not going to be successful working together, and I don't want to waste anymore of your time. I honor that 100%, and I'm sure you can find someone who can solve this problem, who can provide that in a way that you can accept. I just know that starting with that question means you're somebody who I'm not going to be able to help, and I have loved getting to know you and I wish you the best of luck. Bye!"

Hang up the phone. They're going to be trouble-makers the entire time. You will regret having them as clients. They can beg you all they want, but your answer should still be no. I promise you, from the bottom of my soul, it will save you money, and it sends a message to the universe that you are only working with action takers who are willing to let you be the alpha.

If they are communicating, "No, I need to run this hour," they're going to tell you the entire time how to solve their problem, which they know doesn't work, but they can't help themselves. They are going to be such a hard client to work with and they will not get results. You will work twice as hard. You will get half the results. Then, at the end of it, they will ask for a refund. You'll be like, "Oh my God, but I worked twice as hard with you than anyone."

If you do not properly start the call, you will most likely not close it. Almost nothing else matters if you haven't gotten that part right.

Part 2: Open your Ears and Your Heart

The next part of the call is the longest part of the call. It tends to take me about 30 minutes. At a high level, what you're doing is you're saying, "Tell me where you are. Tell me where you want to be. What do you believe is the problem? Why haven't you solved this problem already?"

Here are some of the specific questions I ask:

- Where are you currently with your book?
- Where do you want to go with your book?
- What does success look like?
- If your book is the most successful thing you did, where will you be a year from now?
- What have you tried to get your book finished and get those outcomes?
- What roadblocks did you face along the way?
- What have you done or invested to overcome those roadblocks?
- What worked, and what didn't work?

- What do you think it's costing you not to have your book?
- Would you have more clients, more free time?
- How much longer are you willing to keep doing it your way?
- Some people have plenty of time for trial and error, are you happy to do that?

In this section, this diagnosis section, your job is to listen.

Ask the questions, keep them focused on diagnosing what the problem is, and decide if you can help solve it. If you can fix this problem, and you're 100% sure they want it fixed, then, you can move to the next stage. One of the things I listen for is why they have failed in the past. If they blame their last coach or consultant, just know, you will be next. Is that the type of client you want?

Most of the time, I'm not even really listening as closely to the words as I am to their energy. I'm listening to what's the problem that I see as the doctor, and what is the dream come true that I hear (in their energy and nonverbal cues) they *really* want. When I really get the problem in their words, and the dream come true in their words, it looks like a little light bulb above my head.

Part 3: Voice Your Idea for Them

To transition to Part 3, I almost always say something like that, "Okay, I totally get it. I have an idea for you. We are now transitioning into the part of the call where I tell you what's going on over here." And, "I help people with your problem, get your dream come true in this amount of time. We can usually do that in nine weeks. I like to do that in a one-day VIP session so we bang it out." Don't give them the dates, don't give them the time, don't give them the cost, don't tell them how many calls they get with you. Don't tell them about your student center or your worksheets. Don't talk to them about meditation. You're going to tell them, "You have a problem. You want this dream come true. I help people get this dream come true. Here's how long it will take. How does that sound? Do you have any questions?"

Make sure you're repeating their words back to them. If you give them your words or wishes for them, instead of describing the gap they just told you they wanted to close, you will, likely, lose the sale. It will sound like you are begging *them* to be your client, instead of the other way around.

You cannot put words in their mouth and close sales. When you get to the idea part, repeat their words. You're not going to describe the program. You're going to lead. Part one, we set the agenda. Part two, do the diagnosis. Part three, have an idea and share with them, can you get them that solution or not. You could end the call right there, if not. If you can help them, tell them, "I can get you this result. What questions do you have for me?"

Part 4: Empower Transformation

Now, they're going to ask you for the logistics. When they do this, *they* are inviting *you* to be their coach — this is totally different than you telling them about your program which is what most coaches and consultants do. They're going to ask you, "How does it work?" Give them the critical details but just the facts, don't sell, don't convince, don't tell them it's awesome, or it works, or you know you can help them.

You wrote a book about the problem and now you are going to apply that book to them.

Continue to probe: "What other questions you have for me?" You are not going to give them the price or sell them anything until they say, "How much is it? How do we start? When do we start? What's the next step?" That is how they will "beg you" to be your client.

Here's the point where you might hit some objections. You're going to give them the logistics. You're going to give them the price, and you're going to say things like, "How does that sound? Do you have any other questions? Are you ready to get started? I would love to see you solve this problem. I've got a space this week. I would love to get you in and get you going."

Remember, anything you do to convince at this point, like, "I really think this would be good for you," is going to scare them away. Your whole mantra for this last part of the call is to just lean the hell back and let them come to you. No pushing. The only thing you're allowed to say is some version of, "Do you have any other questions? Can I answer any other questions? Are you ready to get going and solving this problem?"

If they raise an objection, you want to have an answer for that.

If they say, "Now isn't the right time for me. I'm super busy with (whatever, my newborn)." I might say: "Listen, I totally get that. I know when I had a newborn, I wasn't ready to step up. The only thing I heard you say was, you needed to do this now because you have a triathlon coming up in six months. I just want to make sure, because there's two things I'm hearing, and I just want to serve you on this call. You either don't want to do the triathlon in six months, or you do, and then you need to solve this problem now. I don't hear another plan. If the timing is wrong, then, you don't really have this problem. We should just take it off your list. Let's consider it done." All of that listening from the diagnosis comes into play at this stage.

Let's say they say, "I have to talk to my husband first." I would be like, "I totally get that ... maybe you guys have an agreement or you need him to be flexible on something else. I'm happy to stay on hold while you call him. It's perfectly fine with me." I just have never seen anyone hang up the phone with me, go talk to their husband or wife, and come back with a yes. For most people, "I want to go talk to my husband" is a very polite way of saying, "No, thank you." What runs through my mind here is something I may share with the prospect, i.e., "I would much rather see you leave with an empowered no, than giving your husband the power, because what we've been talking about the whole time, in a way, is that your husband holds the power and you need to find a way to establish your own identity and your own career path. Now, we're just giving that away to him again, and I can't, in good conscience, let you do that. What you've told me is you want to claim your space, you want to claim your power, now is the time to do that, and you need to be the one responsible for getting this return on investment."

"You told me earlier, you want to earn $10,000 a month. This $2,000 investment, if you go to your husband and say, 'Hey, I made this investment because here's what I'm going to do.' That holds you accountable in a totally different way than if you give him all the power. I would rather you just say, 'No, thank you. I don't actually want to establish my own power and make $10,000 a month. I would rather keep giving my power to my husband, that's what feels good for me.'"

The way you respond to the objections has everything to do with what you learned in the diagnosis, and what you've observed in your prospect on the call.

You have now learned the L.O.V.E. Method for closing sales. If you follow these four steps, and price your program accordingly, you will end up turning about one in four prospects into clients.

If you are closing better than one in four, I recommend raising your prices by 10-20%. If you
are closing fewer than one in ten, I recommend
re-reading this chapter, listening back to your
sales calls, and perhaps taking some additional
sales training. Almost certainly, you are trying
to "sell" your prospect on why he or she "should"
work with you, and that is a common mistake
that is easily fixable.

It won't surprise you to know my first advice to
Theosophia was to raise her prices. That filled
in some of the extra revenue she wanted, which
enabled her to invest in getting her message
to more spiritual healers. When she raised her
prices, she started to get those Nos. And Nos are
great, because they create space for even more
aligned clients that get even better results. Being
willing to let some good candidates go to make
space for great ones is how movements quickly
get momentum and reach a tipping point. That's
the power of selling with L.O.V.E.

CHAPTER 8

Love 'Em More

Many coaches and consultants follow a launch
style business model. The way it works is they
will buy a bunch of ads to build up their list.
Then they offer their list a free webinar where
they make a pitch. There is a (falsely imposed)
window to purchase whatever they are selling
and the sooner (or later) you buy the more
bonuses you get. I've had the whole process
explained to me no fewer than a dozen times
and every time, I am cursed with a bad case of
situational narcolepsy. I just can't keep my eyes
open it sounds so exhausting.

The list is mostly burned out by the end of these launch shenanigans, and so when the coach wants to launch again, they have to go through the whole exhausting process from the start. They end up with a massive list of non-buyers which seems to give them the credibility to do speaking events and telesummits and podcast interviews where they don't really get clients or help anyone, but I think it soothes their ego.

I probably wouldn't have a problem with any of this if it led to hope, healing, transformation, or just generally making the world a better place. Sadly, it doesn't. These coaches then have massive refund rates, and even the clients who don't refund their purchases often never open the course or take any action. Instead the client feels guilty for spending money and not using the product. Instead of bringing hope and healing, the coach has created space for shame and guilt to thrive.

I know this model works for many people and if that's you, God Bless. This is just one perspective. But to me, in order to grow and fund a movement that matters and to leave the world more beautiful than you found it, there is only one business model that makes sense: Love your prospects. Love your clients more.

And let me just go ahead and define what I mean by love for you. To love a prospect you need to *see* them, to *hear* them, and to *feel* them. You have to "seek first to understand, and then be understood." You aren't trying to *sell* them something. Your business has key performance indicators. Those are numbers. But your clients aren't numbers. They are actual humans, with actual families, and actual dreams. They aren't transactions in a log book.

Your responsibility to your business is to make something sellable and sell it. But your responsibility to your client, in my opinion, is to get them the result you promised. Your focus is to close the gap between where they are and where they want to be. And if you can't do that, you should not have extended an offer.

But here is the funny thing about life: We don't stop dreaming when our dreams come true.

The Dream After the Dream

My clients come to me because they want to write a book. If I make them an offer, they will get that dream. It's as good as done. With over 400 authors, I've only had three not finish their books, and one of those people died. We have a better than 99% success rate. But I'm not gonna lie: I stack the deck! I just don't make offers to people whose dream I can't make come true, in almost every case.

When they are standing on the mountain top, book in hand, dream fulfilled, you would think that would be the moment we hug and part ways. But that's not what happens. Instead, I watch as their pupils get larger and it dawns on them:

Oh fuck, now I actually have to market this thing!

Now, if my clients were just commodities, maybe I wouldn't care. But it turns out, I fell in love with them way back on the sales call. We've journeyed together to make their dream come true. We've weathered a lot of storms together. Writing a book in nine weeks is not for the weak-willed. And now, this actual human that I actually love, has a new dream that I know how to help them get too. After all, I've generated over $10,000,000 from books I've marketed in the last four years alone. I really don't know anyone else in the world who could help them take their book and use it to fill their coaching or consulting business faster or more effectively.

And so, I have a second book marketing offer that I *only* sell to successful book writing clients. In that program, I teach these new authors how to use their book to grow their business and hold them accountable to implementing the plans we create together.

This is the model I recommend for you too. What is the *new dream* that is created when you help your clients solve the problem they have when they meet you?

Finding New Customers Is Expensive

There are two marketing concepts you need to know to really understand the business model I want to teach you.

Cost per acquisition, where you calculate the money you spend to get a new customer in the door.

Life time value, which is the total revenue you can expect to make from the customer.

Hopefully it won't surprise you to learn that if you cost per acquisition (CPA) is *more* than your life time value (LTV), you are definitely not funding your movement. In fact, your CPA should be about 10-20% of your LTV.

Say your cost per acquisition to get a client is $1000, and your program is $1000. What you discover here is you don't make any money, right? But let's say your program is $1000, but that for clients who have a new dream at the end of the program, you offer a more comprehensive follow up program that is $10,000. And let's say 50% of your clients buy this second offer. Now your CPA is $1,000 but your LTV is $6,000. That's a 6X return on your investment. I challenge you to find any stock that returns at that rate!

The 10X ATM

Picture walking into the center of your town, and you stick $1,000 in an envelope. You put it into the ATM machine, and the ATM machine gives you $6,000 back. How often would you use this ATM machine? If you had to walk uphill in the rain, but the ATM machine was open today, would you go to the ATM machine? Yes, you would!

And this is the sort of ATM machine we want to build in your living room, or your home office if you have one.

There are other business models, but hands down, by far, this is the most effective way to build a 6x, or even a 10x ATM in your living room.

Now, not surprisingly, it can be a difficult ATM to build. Who the fuck would let you build a 10x ATM in your living room without drama? Think of how it could be used if it didn't require you to actually do some emotional work on yourself to build this. But the business tactics themselves are not that difficult. I've covered many of them in this book. The bigger challenge is the personal growth and leadership skills required for this kind of momentum. That's why a business coach alone won't get you to your goals. You must go deep and do your own work on your blocks and limitations if you want this ATM at your house.

I will say, if you believe in changing the world and have always wanted to reach more people and make a bigger difference, it sure is handy!

What Funding a Movement Requires

The unfair advantage of this particular business model I am teaching in this chapter, is that you have more money to acquire customers than if you have to acquire customers for 10-20% of a single program. If you only have a budget of $100 - $200 to get a new customer, it will make significantly harder to get customers than if you have $600 or even $1000.

Most people I know who run low-dollar, launch-based businesses, are running so close to their margins they don't have anything left over to fund a movement.

It might be possible with that model to build a small lifestyle business, but it isn't going to really fund a movement. Your very first responsibility is to decide if you just want to focus on a tiny lifestyle business that gets your bills paid, or if you want a business that is not only sold out but gives you time and money to reach a bigger audience.

In your follow up product, you don't necessarily need to teach anything new. Most second level programs are about accountability and implementation. The question to ask yourself is: What is the best way for your clients to implement what they learned in your program?

If they already have a plan to implement what they have learned from you, or if they can look you in the eye and say they don't want to implement the plan, then let them go with love. It's only your job to listen and serve if you can.

This is a totally different model of business than most coaches, healers, and consultants ever learn. It is quite standard in most other industries, however. And you have to understand if you're building a 10x ATM in your living room, it won't happen overnight. I promise you: It's so worth it. Expect this to take a year of concentrated effort. Don't be entitled and think it should happen overnight. But it's worth the focus so you can fund your movement and do what you intend to make the biggest possible impact on this planet, as fast as possible.

CHAPTER 9

Iterate and Optimize

Brian's stood behind me and placed his hands on my hips.

"Now I want you to hinge here at the waist, grab the matte with your hands, and push the mat to the other side of the gym – as quickly as you can."

It was early. I was cranky. And this just seemed so pointless. I did not want to push the mat that way! Could I just carry it? Everything about having a personal trainer was annoying me, not the least of which was the fact I had not lost any weight from working out, and we were 16 sessions in. I had reached a tipping point.

Working out was not for me, or maybe Brian just wasn't a good trainer. Anyway, I had my mind made up, I was going to quit at the end of the session.

I pushed the damn mat and delivered my carefully rehearsed speech: "Brian, it's been 8 weeks since I started training with you. I have come every week, twice a week, and I've done everything you have asked to the best of my ability. But I haven't lost any weight and working out hasn't gotten any easier. I still dread every exercise, and everything you give me is hard for me."

The corners of Brian's mouth contracted and his cheeks slid up, making crow's feet appear around his eyes. "Wait, did you think working out was supposed to get *easier*? I make the workouts harder every session. Your workouts should *never* get easier."

I was confused. It looked like working out was easy for a gym rat, and it sure felt hard for me. I thought working out more would make me stronger, and therefore the workouts would be more enjoyable. I had been willing to stick with exercise for 8 weeks, as long as there was a promise of a future where working out was fun and easy – and made me feel healthy and strong.

Brian's words weren't making sense.

"So, if you always make it harder, when will I be able to enjoy it?" I asked, trying to get inside the mindset of fit people.

"Oh, that's easy," Brian said. "When you decide to."

Outside circumstances were not going to change. The workout was going to get harder every single time. And yet, I had the power to decide to enjoy it. Even if I wasn't losing weight? *Huh?*

That day, I picked ambiguity. I didn't quit, but I didn't fully commit, either. I wanted to lose more weight, and I wanted to be stronger. Brian said I had been getting stronger, and I could tell my clothes were fitting better, but the number of the scale didn't move. I didn't realize I had gotten stronger because I was doing harder things. Did that count?

Maybe he was just a slick salesman trying to pull one over on me. *How could I know?*

I called my weight loss coach to try to make sense of all of this. I thought she would ask for stats like my weight by day, or a breakdown of the workouts we had been doing, so I had all of that prepared but she didn't care about the details.

"What do you *want* the reason to be that you work out?"

I thought it was to lose weight and get stronger. But now I had a different answer: "Because it challenges me to show up and take care of myself."

"Then don't fight the challenges or wish them away. Don't expect working out to do something for you that you aren't willing to do for yourself."

I stopped checking the scale, and I met Brian back in the gym three days later, on schedule. I was angry I hadn't lost weight, but I'd also noticed that I'd been eating twice as much on days when I went to the gym.

Why? Because doing physical things made me uncomfortable. And my solution for feeling uncomfortable, of course, was to eat. Eating more than my body required for fuel was what caused me to not lose weight. Not losing weight was why I was going to quit personal training, because it didn't work.

But *it wasn't* the personal training that was not working for me. It was *my brain*. I was trying to make Brian responsible to make me feel good when I worked out. I was trying to make Brian responsible to overcome my choice to overeat.

When I changed the *reason*, I was choosing working out – from losing weight and getting strong to showing up and taking care of myself – I took accountability for the outcomes I was getting.

If I wanted to enjoy working out more, that wasn't Brian's responsibility, it was mine.

If I wanted to lose weight, eating less wasn't Brian's responsibility, it was mine.

Building a business is like going to the gym. On one level, it may seem like your goal is to make more money and help more people. But the deeper question is the more important one to answer.

What do you want the reason to be that you built a business?

Are you expecting your business to do something for you that you aren't willing to do for yourself?

I can give you my reason for building a business: Because it challenges all areas of personal growth and development – often all at the same time!

The money, and the satisfaction of helping people, is reward itself – and each is a fantastic one – but it's not the reason I do the work. And therefore, I don't expect the work to be easy.

The steps for using a book to get clients, make a difference for readers, and generate tens of thousands of dollars in revenue aren't hard. I've taught many of them in this book, but like the steps for losing weight and getting stronger (aka eat less, exercise more), the difference between those who fail and those who succeed is determined by the mindset of the person who wants the goal.

If you have the belief that doing 10-20 hours a week of awareness activities should be easy, you might be disappointed. If you have the belief that you should make money and then invest in your business, you will be disappointed for sure. If you have the belief that just because you *can* help someone dramatically they *should* buy from you, you are going to be disappointed.

But if you have a belief like, "*This is going to be hard and that's exactly why I'm doing it*," then you can have so much fun!

The fastest path to a sold-out practice is detaching from the need to have a sold-out practice. I know it's frustratingly counterintuitive, but once you can accept this, the next thing I'm going to teach you is going to be a lot more fun to learn.

Taking action to market your book and create a business where clients are begging to work with you is going to bring up resistance, and our goal is not to be sad about the resistance, nor allow it to derail us from our work. There isn't some day in the future where you don't feel negative emotions.

Feelings are going to come up, so how you handle them is actually much more important than trying to get them to not show up or trying to get out of feeling them. Avoiding is never going to work anyway, so we might as well just get good at feeling and managing them.

Earlier in the book, I explained how you need to let things run for 90 days to find out if they're working. Now, if something is a total and unmitigated disaster, I am not suggesting you keep doing something that is wildly ineffective for 90 days, bash your head against a wall, and miss a quarter. If you are changing tactics you have to be 100% sure it's not because you are trying to avoid feeling negative feelings.

One of the ways I know I'm making a change for the right reasons is that there is no drama surrounding it, and it feels sort of boring. Going back to my example in the gym, recall how I was all nervous to tell Brian I was quitting and then I was feeling ambiguous and confused. That's not what it will feel like if you should switch something you are doing within the quarter. And you should not make any changes at all until you can address the drama that surrounds it. Then once you figure out why you are having negative feelings, you can make a decision about changing your marketing tactics from a clean place. Until it feels neutral, you do not need to take action.

As an example, say you are doing a webinar. You might be wondering if you change it up, will more people attend, will they stay longer, will they convert at a higher rate. But you don't really have enough data to decide. Give it at least 90 days before you make changes to adjust something that may be working well with just a little more time.

And when you do start to iterate and optimize, you won't want to change everything at once. In fact, I recommend making no more than one change per week. Make a habit to ask yourself, what's the *one* most important thing I can fix this week? Each week you are going to become an expert on one new problem in your business. That's why we want them running wrong, rather than ripping everything apart and rebuilding it.

Burning down the fucking barn is a terrible way to run a business. Do not burn down the barn. People are living there! Let's just get new windows. Then we can just replace the floorboards. Or how about we buy some rugs? Each week, we're going to change one thing about the barn, and eventually you will have a new barn, and it will be beautiful, and you will love it. We did not need to burn it down and kill people, or at least make them homeless and alone, okay?

What's your problem this week?

The number one problem I see is that people aren't crystal clear on what problem they are solving. The biggest problem in your business is the one that is blocking your revenue.

"I don't have enough clients." That is not a problem anyone can help you solve. It's too big. You must unwind the Gordian knot. That is your primary job as CEO. The only thing you can't ever hire someone for is to untie the Gordian knot of knowing what your actual business is, and what your actual problems are.

If you don't want to do this part, this is a great reason to get, and love, having a job. There are jobs everywhere. There are wonderful people who are happy to be employees. Having faced some of the ramp-up to entrepreneurship, now you will understand part of why you get paid so much less as an employee than you could as an entrepreneur.

Once you identify a specific problem, you can hire people to do those tasks. Until you know what the *actual* problem is, anyone you hire will disappoint you, and you will want a refund and question their competence. (Kind of like I did with Brian, the trainer.)

You are the problem. *You* are the variable. This is true for most core business problems!

Good news: Solving your problems is actually quite straightforward when you approach it this way. No problem, on its own, is actually that hard to solve. And most of your problems *are* in your reach to move toward solutions.

Here are some of the most common problems that people have in their businesses to help you identify:

1. Awareness (how people hear of you). You may realize, after you decided speaking was

what you were going to do, that it's killing your schedule, and you hate it, and it's taking energy away. Great! Keep booking speaking gigs until you can identify and test a better alternative. This is your obligation to the company.

2. Lead Generation (how people raise their hand to show interest). What is the actual problem with lead gen? Are people not raising their hand? Are they not showing interest? Are you getting a lot of hand raisers, but they're not converting? What is the actual problem?

3. Sales cycle (how people go from knowing you and liking you to trusting you with their money). Do you have a sales cycle problem, or is it a problem with your emails? Do you have the right data? It doesn't need to change until we have the data. If you are not at 10 sales calls yet, that's not your biggest problem yet. Once you are getting better at sales, it is going to be your number one goal – because if you can improve that close rate, you can scale faster.

4. Product (having powerful products that get results). Make sure your product gets results. Do you need to optimize your product? That means you have plenty of awareness, you have plenty of leads, you're converting them, you have clients – and they aren't getting results. Make sure that is where you are before you change your product.

5. Delivering your offer (operations and scaling). Are you having trouble keeping up with demand? Do you need better processes and procedures to get more done in less time? Do you need help?

6. Managing the drama (the role of story). Always stay focused on keeping all your stories straight about what the *real* problem is instead of the imagined or created one!

This is how you optimize and iterate a business. You can do this, it's not any harder than going to the gym. But you will never succeed unless you are doing it for the right reason. So make sure you know why you are going the entrepreneurship path in the first place, and what you are getting yourself into. It is a great way to make a difference, but it comes with its own challenges.

CHAPTER 10

Manage the Drama

One of the main reasons why I chose to overeat most of my life is because it made it easier for me not to feel my feelings. I think Brooke Castillo explains this really well, in that she describes your body like a like a glass jar. Imagine you put a coin into a glass jar and shake it. There's going to be a lot of noise, right? It's almost like I'm making a musical instrument. If you were to fill that glass jar up with cotton balls, and then put the coin in there and shake it, you would not hear the same level of noise. The cotton balls would be buffering that sound. The reason why I ate was to soften that noise.

The coin, of course, represents your feelings. I didn't want to hear all that noise, so I ate (food, not cotton balls). It worked very well. I am super impressed with my ability to come up with that solution.

What this led to, as a side effect of drowning out the feelings, was an extra 150 pounds of weight I did not require. In fact, I was extremely uncomfortable in my body because I was stuffing it all the time. I was like busting out of my body. Maybe you can relate to some feelings making your coins jingle loudly in your own glass jar. Maybe you have your own cotton balls, whether they be food or something else. But an *emotion* is just a *sensation* passing through your body. It's not the end of the world – no one comes and takes your children away because your feelings are unpleasant. You don't die. You can actually *feel* a feeling and not be harmed. But before I learned this, it definitely felt like I was going to die, and so I would stuff things into the jar.

One day, my coach, Brooke Castillo took me to a ropes course in Lake Tahoe. On this ropes course, we were challenged to climb high things. When you climb a high thing, you very often feel a sensation in your body, especially if you're 300 pounds. There was this particular activity on the course: a telephone pole, which we had to climb. We'd get to the top of the telephone pole, stand on it, and then parkour-style, jump onto another telephone pole which was approximately a mile away. I think it was really more like two feet away, but it definitely felt like a mile to me, and we were to leap from one onto the next. If you fell, you would die, which is why I don't want to feel my feelings. (Really, we were harnessed and on like a carabiner, so if you fell everything would actually be fine, but it did not feel that way to me.)

I climbed the telephone pole. Three hundred fifty pounds, by the way, is a lot of weight to carry up a telephone pole. I kept climbing, despite the fact that I did not want to do this, until I got to the top rung on the pole — at which point, I was supposed to stand up on the top of the pole.

I was so proud of myself for making it to the top. I really felt like I did my best. Every single step up the pole was a struggle. I was feeling my fucking feelings, but I kept climbing – I didn't quit.

When I went to stand on the pole, I had a problem, in that my fat rolls were blocking my leg from bending at the angle that was required to get up there. Part of me was trying to find another way to stand on the top of the pole. (Maybe kneel first?) But I was also thinking, *If I get up there I am for sure going to die, because if I stand on it, then I'm going to have to jump to the other pole.*

Can you hear like the jangling of my thoughts here?

As I explained to Brooke, "I totally get that other people could stand on the top of this telephone pole. I watched other people do this. But for me, it is clearly different, because of the shape of my body."

Brooke wasn't buying it, yet I kept arguing. "No, I

understand it *can* be done, but obviously *I* can't do it. Let me show you my fat rolls. *See?* My leg can't do that. I'm not flexible."

Brooke stood at the bottom of the pole yelling up to me. *You can definitely do it!*

I yelled back. Let me just explain one more time.

I had all the reasons why I couldn't do it, and she finally said, "Look. It's totally up to you if you want to do this or not. It is not going to change my life. You stand on the pole or not. Your call."

I said, "I totally get that, but I would like you to acknowledge that I have done my best – like, even though I didn't jump, I have done my best. Please acknowledge that."

Brooke disagreed. "Your best would be jumping."

She would not let me off the hook. But I came back down the pole anyway. Without her blessing.

Later, when I tried to explain why I couldn't physically do what she asked, I really wanted her to acknowledge that I was right. I just had a physical limitation, plain and simple.

"Argue for your limitations, and you get to keep them," she said.

"No, no, I'm not arguing for my limitations. I wanted to get at the top but I couldn't do it."

"I'm not buying it," she said. "If your son's life was in jeopardy if you didn't jump, you would have figured out a way."

I knew she was right. I actually could have done it. I wanted to explain the ergonomics of my body.

But if somebody was at the bottom of the pole with a gun to Jesse's head...well...I would have stood on the pole and jumped. Which means I was capable of it, and it was only my thoughts that would not allow me to do it.

There is a point at which I won't be able to teach you another tool. I will have nothing left to give. Because the person who wants the result has to just do it. The only person who can do it, is you.

You are the only one who can stop arguing for your limitations, because if you want them, or if you fear the discomfort of living without them, you get to keep them.

When you move forward with creating the kind of business that will get clients begging to work with you, you will be in an amazing new place with a new energy and lots of exciting stuff happening – and that will bring up more beautiful resistance of its own.

This process of becoming the leader of your movement – stepping on to a bigger stage where clients are begging for the chance to work with you – isn't about reaching the top of the mountain and relaxing. You know what you can see from the top of the mountain? *More mountains.* With each of those tactical steps in getting there, a million things are going to go wrong, and they're supposed to! Those things that go wrong are going to bring up feelings in you that you will not want to feel. Then to avoid feeling them, your thoughts will be telling you either stop doing the tactic, do a different tactic, or just decide you should give up now, because no tactics will ever work for you – ever. Those are the feelings we want to manage, but the truth is, they never, ever, *ever* go away. That's the bad news. They actually only get bigger. The good news about the fact that they never go away is that, as long as you don't quit, you get much better at managing them.

In this book I've given you a list of possible awareness activities. There is an awareness activity that works for you. I hundred-percent promise. It kind of doesn't matter which one you choose, as long as your pick one of them, which is why I want you to commit to that action for 90 days. I know that way it will bring up the negative emotions you are trying to avoid feeling and working through that emotional minefield is the secret to your ongoing success.

If we can catch these thoughts and change them, your tactics will end up changing if they need to, but for the right reasons, and with no drama attached.

I look forward to you failing at your landing page. I look forward to you embarrassing yourself at a networking event. I look forward to you having a terrible sales call, where you start off by giving the price and don't close any sales. And the reason I look forward to all of those things, even though it sounds like a terrible experience, is that is how you will be learning how to manage your thoughts, and to come out of imperfections (and even humiliations) with the full knowledge that you are still the best in the world at what you do for who you do it. That is going to develop your confidence and your ability to stay clear in your purpose – in other words, the way you get clients begging to work with you.

You are at the top of the telephone pole. Do not stop before you stand on the telephone pole. You cannot go back in time and recapture this moment. This is the life blood of your future. This is your future self out here, stand and jump!

CHAPTER 11

Baby, It's You.

Back in the 90s, I once worked on a book about lottery winners, and proceeded to interview 80 lottery winners. In the process, I learned 79 of the 80 not only lost all the money they won in the lottery, but they lost even more than that. The only person I talked to who hadn't lost all their money was somebody who already had a lot of family money. They had a wealth manager in place. They had already spent a lot of time on money mindset. And they were ready for more money, so they were able to take that money and grow it. By the time I interviewed them for that book, it had been about 10 years since their lottery winnings. They basically had multiplied 10x what they won in the lottery through investment, while almost everyone else lost it. Those 79 of 80 not only lost more money than they had won, but they also had lost lawsuits, homes, businesses, and even lost family members.

Why? Because they hadn't built up the emotional muscle to be the person who had that money.

This is what I want you to know about getting people begging to be your client. It isn't about the tactics, though there are many in this book you can apply to your business (and I hope you do!). Know this: The tactics alone won't work. The tactics will backfire if you don't *also* become the person who has the result *before* you get it.

Here's the secret: Everything your brain wants to do, remember to keep you alive, is to avoid becoming that person. Avoiding discomfort and change. Shedding the skin that served you in a painful process that includes feeling a lot of difficult feelings. Those feelings will make you more uncomfortable. And look, you don't *have* to do the difficult emotional work, or process how you're sabotaging your growth, and start choosing the thoughts and behaviors of the next level of success. You could just stay right where you are. Remember, the brain thinks it won if you simply woke up the next morning. Whatever you did yesterday, you are programming your brain for, "Oh, do that again. We woke up. We're alive."

If last week you went out there, and launched an imperfect webinar in some fashion – say you got some people to sign up, or you didn't, or not as many as you wanted, or your technology broke, or you had some weird Internet troll calling you names, whatever came up that felt like *risk* – and it left you feeling *uncomfortable*, that's because your brain was busy trying to stop that shit from coming up. Your brain was saying, "We might die. What if that Internet troll comes and kills us in the night?"

It's also true when you simply did it anyway, and then went to sleep and woke up in the morning, that is reprogramming your brain to be the person who has the outcome you want. Whatever happened, as long as you did it, you won. Give yourself a pat on the back!

One of the tools I share with my clients is to always have a list of rewards that you will give yourself for doing the hard stuff. It can be as simple as watching an episode of some trashy reality TV show midday or buying a nice pen.

It's not that I care if you get a reward, it's that habit programs your brain and it says, "We lived. We can do hard things. Even better, we got something we wanted out of it." Find ways to reward your brain. That's really the goal here. That's why the key that determines your success isn't the tactics, but your ability to manage the drama around action, and keep moving forward. The way you tell yourself we did that is, "Now, have the Netflix binge." We don't Netflix binge to avoid feeling our feelings. We Netflix binge to reward ourselves for feeling our feelings, and surviving, and taking the steps to change.

I want you to continually reward yourself for taking action, because it reprograms your brain to say, "This is safe. We're not going to die. We can do hard things. We can put ourselves out there and fuck shit up, and nobody dies, and this is actually fun, and we get rewards."

When you listen back to one of your sales calls, I want you to reward yourself with a nap or a mid-day meditation, or something you find totally delicious. I love smoothies, but I really hate the process of having to go to the store, buy the ingredients, blend it, clean the blender. Give yourself an hour and a half, after you've listened to a sales call, to make a killer smoothie and clean up after it, and then just enjoy it. You have nowhere else to be. You will think that it's about the smoothie, and it's not about the smoothie at all, it is about integrating and reflecting on what you've learned and listened to. That's actually work, you can count it as work time. It will lead to clients. It will lead to revenue. It will lead to funding your movement. It will lead to people begging to be your client.

An author who has people begging to work with her is spending considerable time getting the word out about her work (we call this awareness); she is frequently offering free content in exchange for contact information (we call these lead magnets); and she is offering to serve those people she can truly help, and with love. Getting to sustainable momentum from zero takes considerable and consistent focus and effort on a few specific activities to attract a few people – just one or two a week – to step through your wee portal.

You have to have the right strategy, and then you have to actually take action on the tactics and optimize them. While in action, you have to manage all the drama that's going to come up. We're not trying to reach a point where your drama never comes up, we're trying to reach a point where this level of drama is so boring that you're ready to move on to the next level of drama. When you look at the amount of drama that the people who have really powerful movements can handle, it's a whole lot more than you can. Turn your focus onto doing the tactics while knowing *I'm not going to feel awesome all the time*, but through this discomfort and growth you get to actually build that muscle up and create your movement.

Earlier in the book I asked, "*What do you want the reason to be for growing your business?*" Money alone won't keep you motivated. For me, the answer is simple: I believe entrepreneurship is the single best way to reach your highest human potential. When you are the best in the world at solving a specific problem, and you know it, you don't have to convince someone to buy from you, you can just love them – and trust they will know what to do.

One of our talent scouts said it best. He said, "I think the real testament to a L.O.VE.ing 'sales' process is when the clients who *don't* buy from you thank you profusely for the process. They feel they have been seen, heard and cared for, they thank you, and may look forward to an opportunity to buy from you in the future."

That's what I want for each of you, to have clients begging you to take their money and knowing they would do it again, 100 times, to have the experience they had with you. You have the strategy, you have the tactics. Now go manage the drama – and make the world a better place.

ACKNOWLEDGMENTS

First, I have to thank the woman who inspired this book's creation with her simple, celebratory post about finishing her own book. The Myrna from the first chapter is Myrna Buckles, the author of *Wigs, Scarves and Lies*. While she lives on the other side of the country, it felt as though she was next to me with every chapter I wrote. Thanks for being so brave and vulnerable, for sharing so generously, and for always being willing to step up and help. You inspire me! And I hope the book I wrote for you will inspire many others as well. Thanks for asking such great questions.

I feel like all my clients are my soulmates, but some soulmate clients happen to live nearby and share a lot of the same interests as I do (like shoes and spas and crystals.) Thank you Nurys for making it so easy and fun to write. Having you next door made it impossible to quit. I love having such a badass recruiting industry rock star as a client, and I'm even more grateful to also be able to call you a friend.

While I was away writing this book, my husband Paul was home, sick, and holding down the fort, er… um… *castle*. Thanks for being there, so I could be 100% here. I am never quite sure what I'd do without you.

My favorite human turned 12 while I was writing this book. Thank you, Jesse, for holding off your birthday celebrations until I finished. You make me proud every day. Thanks for being my greatest teacher and one of the kindest people I've ever met. I love you!

Love beams of gratitude to Mila, Sofia, Lauti and the rest of my family – and to the entire team at The Author Incubator; especially Heather "Big Love" Russell, our head Talent Scout and the torch bearer for our LOVE Method of Sales, and Cal Misener, who gave me the ending for the book at the exact moment I needed it.

If it weren't for Dr. Diva Nagula and the entire staff at www.TheIVDoc.com pumping me full of vitamins so I would be healthy enough to write, this book could not exist. If you have never tried IV hydration therapy and you find yourself run down from jet lag and a cold just before you have committed to write a book, I highly recommend looking into it. I've never felt better or had more energy!

Finally, I'd like to acknowledge the incredible hospitality of The Salamander Resort & Spa, where this book was written.

ABOUT THE AUTHOR

Dr. Angela E. Lauria is the founder of The Author Incubator™ and creator of the Difference Process™ for writing a book that matters. In 2017, The Author Incubator was ranked #285 on the Inc. 500 fastest growing companies and #260 on Entrepreneur Magazine's Entrepreneur 360. Dr. Angela won the 2017 Coach/Mentor of the Year Award and her program, The Author's Way was named Coaching Program of the Year by the Stevie Awards. Dr. Angela was also named, by Entrepreneur Magazine, as one of the top 10 most inspiring entrepreneurs to watch – one of only 2 women on the list.

Dr. Angela hosts ^Page UP^, a podcast which provides inspiration and information for authors who want to leverage a book to reach more people with their message. Helping people free their inner author since 1994, she has helped over 300 authors-in transformation write, publish, and promote their books. Her clients have been seen everywhere from Vanity Fair to O Magazine to the Today Show, and their books have been responsible for over $10 million in cumulative revenue.

She is the author of Make 'Em Beg to Publish Your Book: How To Reach A Larger Audience & Make A Full-Time Income In The Extremely Overcrowded World of Personal Development, The Incubated Author: 10 Steps to Start a Movement with Your Message and The Difference: 10 Steps To Writing A Book That Matters. She lives at The Author Castle in McLean, Virginia with her husband Paul, her son Jesse, and their Castle cats, Chaos and Princess Feathers McFuzz Bucket.

ABOUT
DIFFERENCE PRESS

Difference Press is the exclusive publishing arm of The Author Incubator, an educational company for entrepreneurs, including life coaches, healers, consultants, and community leaders, looking for a comprehensive solution to get their books written, published, and promoted. Its founder, Dr. Angela Lauria, has been bringing to life the literary ventures of hundreds of authors-in-transformation since 1994.

A boutique-style self-publishing service for clients of The Author Incubator, Difference Press boasts a fair and easy-to-understand profit structure, low-priced author copies, and author-friendly contract terms. Most importantly, all of our #incubatedauthors maintain ownership of their copyright at all times.

Let's Start a Movement with Your Message
In a market where hundreds of thousands of books are published every year and are never

heard from again, The Author Incubator is different. Not only do all Difference Press books reach Amazon bestseller status, but all of our authors are actively changing lives and making a difference.

Since launching in 2013, we've served over 500 authors who came to us with an idea for a book and were able to write it and get it self-published in less than 6 months. In addition, more than 100 of those books were picked up by traditional publishers and are now available in book stores. We do this by selecting the highest quality and highest potential applicants for our future programs.

Our program doesn't just teach you how to write a book - our team of coaches, developmental editors, copy editors, art directors, and marketing experts incubate you from book idea to published bestseller, ensuring that the book you create can actually make a difference in the world. Then we give you the training you need to use your book to make the difference in the world, or to create a business out of serving your readers.

Are You Ready to Make a Difference?

You've seen other people make a difference with a book. Now it's your turn. If you are ready to stop watching and start taking massive action, go to http://theauthorincubator.com/apply/.

"Yes, I'm ready!"

OTHER BOOKS BY DR. ANGELA LAURIA

 The Difference: 10 Steps to Write a Book that Matters (Released: December 13, 2014)

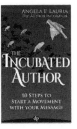 The Incubated Author: 10 Steps to Start a Movement (Released: January 17, 2016)

 Make 'Em Beg to Publish Your Book: How To Reach A Larger Audience & Make A Full-Time Income In The Extremely Overcrowded World of Personal Development (Released: May 15, 2017)

OTHER BOOKS BY
DIFFERENCE PRESS

Your Key to the Akashic Records: Fulfill Your Soul's Highest Potential

by Jiayuh Chyan

...But I'm Not Racist!: Tools for Well-Meaning Whites

by Kathy Obear

Who the Fuck Am I To Be a Coach: A Warrior's Guide to Building a Wildly Successful Coaching Business From the Inside Out

by Megan Jo Wilson

A Graceful Goodvye: A New Outlook on Death

by Susan B. Mercer

Lasting Love At Last: The Gay Guide To Attracting the Relationship of Your Dreams

by Amari Ice

Finding Time to Lead: Seven Practices to Unleash Outrageous Potential

by Leslie Peters

THANKS FOR READING

When I talk to traditional publishers and agents about The Author Incubator, they are gobsmacked by the incredibly high percentage of our authors who have generated $250,000 or more from their books. These numbers are easily ten times what they would expect new, non-fiction authors to attain.

I created a companion class for this book, which can be found over atQuarterMillionBook.com. If you want to understand more about how to use your book to get clients who are begging you to work with them, check out the training and let me know what you think on your favorite social media site.

Facebook - https://www.facebook.com/TheAuthorIncubator/

Twitter - https://twitter.com/authorincubator

Instagram - https://www.instagram.com/authorincubator/

Linked In - https://www.linkedin.com/company/1589902/

76910489R00110

Made in the USA
Middletown, DE
16 June 2018